D1407451

GROWING OLDER
WITH CF

A Handbook for Adults

Copyright for material from other sources included in this book:

'Upper Respiratory Tract' illustration, from Cystic Fibrosis: The Facts by Ann Harris and Maurice Super (3rd edition 1995). © Ann Harris and Maurice Super 1995. Reproduced by permission of Oxford University Press.

'Sex and CF', from Input, a magazine produced by adults with cystic fibrosis (Issue 26, Summer 2000). © Sam Hillyard 2000. Reproduced by permission of Sam Hillyard, author.

ISBN: 0-9540536-0-5

Typesetting by
The Phoenix Setting Company
Portsmouth, Hampshire.

Printed and bound by
Ashford Colour Press Limited
Gosport, Hampshire.

Growing Older with CF was published by the Cystic Fibrosis Trust, UK through an educational grant from Solvay Healthcare Limited as a service to adults with CF and their carers.

Editorial Team and Contributors

The individuals listed below provided invaluable information and guidance during the development of the UK edition of this handbook, based on the original book by the same title produced in the USA by Solvay Pharmaceuticals, Inc.

> Stuart Elborn, Consultant Physician, Adult CF Unit, Belfast City Hospital.
>
> Kevin Webb, Clinical Director of Bradbury Adult CF Unit, Wythenshawe Hospital, Manchester.
>
> Steve Conway, Lead Clinician in CF Services, St James's University Hospital and Seacroft Hospital, Leeds.
>
> Alistair Duff, Clinical Psychologist, Seacroft Hospital, Leeds.
>
> Helen Oxley, Clinical Psychologist, Bradbury Adult CF Unit, Wythenshawe Hospital, Manchester.
>
> Teresa Jacklin, Chairperson, Adult CF Association.
>
> Jim Littlewood OBE, Paediatrican and Chairman CF Trust Research and Medical Advisory Committee.
>
> Members of the Cystic Fibrosis Trust and their Publications Advisory Committee.
>
> Members of Solvay Healthcare Ltd.

Thanks are also due to Jenny Bryan, who took all the comments and contributions, and used them to adapt and extend the original text.

The Editorial Team are very grateful for the contributions to the UK edition made by the following individuals on their personal experiences of living with cystic fibrosis:

> Andrea Armitage; Joanne Baker; Sheredan Birch; Helen Douglas; Sam Hillyard; Teresa Jacklin; Lesley Saunders, David West, *Anon*

and to:

> Peter Lewis, Senior Lecturer, Department of Medical Sciences, University of Bath, for the chart and information on survival in CF.
>
> David Sheppard, Lecturer, Department of Physiology, University of Bristol, for the illustration on CFTR function.

The Editorial Team extend their thanks to the people with CF, their parents, carers and members of the medical profession working in CF who provided invaluable help during the production of this book.

Finally, thanks are due to the team who produced the original US version which inspired the production of the current UK edition.

When the Cystic Fibrosis Trust was formed in 1964, it would have been unthinkable to write a book-called 'Growing Older With Cystic Fibrosis: A Handbook for Adults' because children with Cystic Fibrosis did not usually grow older. Indeed, they had a struggle to reach adolescence.

Thankfully, all that has changed. We now have adults with Cystic Fibrosis who are doctors, lawyers, sportsmen and women, teachers, secretaries, parents, occasionally grandparents and dare I mention even the odd prisoner, but then not all adults with CF are angels!

The Cystic Fibrosis Trust recognises that the commitment and dedication of the clinical teams and researchers has helped to make this improvement in quality and length of life possible. However, the real thanks have to go to the families of CF children who work so hard to keep their children well, and the adolescents and young adults who accept or 'put up with' a gruelling and time consuming schedule of treatment to stay as well as possible. For many, the demanding nature of daily treatment is worse than the fact that CF is life threatening. Most of them do it – or at least some of it, because they have hopes and dreams for the future. They want to live to make their contribution, have a family, have some fun along the way and grow old gracefully or disgracefully – as we all do.

With adult CF patients have come new physical challenges. They are usually faced with remarkable fortitude and good humour but frustration, fear and anxiety understandably play a part in growing up with CF. The ideal package of treatment to maintain best possible health is recommended by the clinical team and is then considered by the teenager or adult with CF.

He or she then reviews the options in the light of what else is happening at the time – the demands of adolescent life with its parties and clubbing, the determination not to jeopardise a promising new relationship because of CF, the commitment to complete that course, get those 'A' levels or degrees and the strong and sometimes overwhelming instinct to have a child. A compromise is reached, either openly in discussion between the patient and the clinical team, or by the patient alone, deciding what he or she thinks is essential and what can be sacrificed.

We must never forget that for most of these 3,500 adults, CF is not their first priority. They are focussed on the same things as all other young people. Adolescents with CF place the same emphasis on the "drugs, sex and rock and roll culture" as do teenagers without CF.

Education, careers, relationships and families loom large at this time too. Sometimes these pre-occupations coincide with a period of poor health, which brings its own anxieties. Parents often feel helpless and excluded at such times; their role must not be undervalued or relegated, but it has to change.

This book provides a factual backdrop to life with CF, both from a physical and psychological perspective. It addresses the sensitive matters of fertility and pregnancy. It also offers practical advice on money matters, housing, holidays and insurance. It doesn't

3

duck the tough issues that come with deteriorating health. It also considers CF from the perspective of those who are not diagnosed until adulthood with a whole new set of challenges and required adaptations.

The Cystic Fibrosis Trust hopes that this book will be used to enable CF to be managed well, in order for life to be lived to the full. Reliable information combined with the experiences of other CF adults, along with the determination, no nonsense approach to life and sense of perspective and humour on the part of those with CF will help keep CF in the background where it belongs.

One day, we will be able to cure CF. Until that day, our objective is to keep everyone with CF as well as possible to make the most of the 'here and now'.

Rosie Barnes
Chief Executive
Cystic Fibrosis Trust

GROWING OLDER WITH CYSTIC FIBROSIS: A HANDBOOK FOR ADULTS

By 2005, there are likely to be as many adults with CF in the UK as there are children. Once a tragic, poorly understood condition from which people died in early childhood, CF is now a serious, chronic but treatable disorder which is presenting new challenges to people with the disease, their families and the medical teams who care for them.

Effective antibiotics, good nutrition, regular physiotherapy and, not least, the combined efforts of committed families and skilled professionals have transformed the outlook for people with CF over the last 30 years.

But there are fresh challenges for the growing numbers of adults with CF. In addition to the lung and digestive problems, adulthood brings new complications, including diabetes, liver disease and osteoporosis, and raises new issues such as contraception, infertility and pregnancy. There are also the emotional stresses and strains of living with a long-term, life threatening condition and its impact on education, careers, relationships and families.

Adults with CF have new and changing needs for medical and other support services. As in many other countries, adult CF services in the UK have lagged behind those for children. In many parts of the country, demand for adult treatment facilities and information resources has grown rapidly, and outstripped available services.

What is available to adults with CF in one area may be quite different from that elsewhere. Some adults get their treatment at large specialist centres, others receive their routine care at their local hospital, and yet others at a combination of specialist and local hospitals. This is not to say that big is automatically better! Small teams of dedicated professionals with a real interest in CF can provide excellent care with limited resources.

However, the CF Trust believes that people with CF deserve the same high standards of care as those with other higher profile, chronic conditions – regardless of where they live. To this end, the Trust produces national guidance on the treatment of the many and varied problems associated with CF in adults and children[1].

Living with CF can be a difficult business, even when support is good. It can be even more challenging when you don't have the information you need to help make decisions about your medical care and social welfare.

This book aims to bridge the gap in knowledge and understanding about what it means to be an adult who also happens to have CF. An adult who wants to lead as normal a working and social life as possible while still having to meet the demands of an intensive, time consuming and intrusive daily treatment schedule.

Cystic fibrosis is an inherited disorder that occurs mainly in people of European origin, but may also affect those of African, Caribbean and Asian descent. In the UK, over 7000 people have CF.

When the Association of CF Adults UK carried out a survey of nearly 2000 adults with CF in 1994, it found that the age range of respondents was 16–71 years. The most common age was 23[2].

In the last 50 years, the outlook for people with CF has improved dramatically (Figure 1), so that most children born with CF today can expect to live into their 30s, 40s and even beyond.

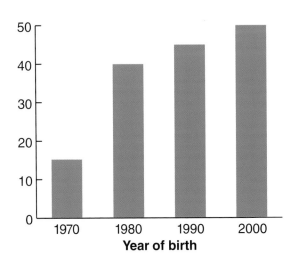

Fig 1. – Actual (1970) and estimated (1980, 1990 & 2000) median survival for UK CF cohorts born in given year.

Many things have played a part in improving life expectancy. We now know far more about the disease itself, and how to treat it. We have better antibiotics and nutritional support, including more effective pancreatic enzyme supplements. We also have more aggressive supportive treatments, administered by teams of different specialists, and we have innovative therapies, such as DNase and other mucus-thinning agents.

We know how important it is to maintain a daily routine of physiotherapy and exercise, and we have the option of lung and heart-lung transplantation for those who are very ill.

How CF affects your body

CF affects many parts of the body, including the lungs, the digestive system, the sweat glands, and the reproductive organs (Figure 2).

But the various medical conditions that make up the disorder which we know as CF are all connected to changes, or mutations, in a single gene. This gene

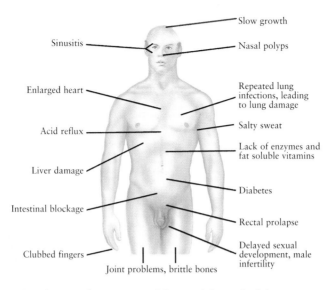

Slow growth

Nasal polyps

Sinusitis

Enlarged heart

Acid reflux

Liver damage

Intestinal blockage

Clubbed fingers

Joint problems, brittle bones

Repeated lung infections, leading to lung damage

Salty sweat

Lack of enzymes and fat soluble vitamins

Diabetes

Rectal prolapse

Delayed sexual development, male infertility

Fig 2. – Signs and symptoms of CF in adults and adolescents.
© SPInc 2000

controls production of a protein called CF trans-membrane conductance regulator (CFTR). The CF gene is therefore correctly called the CFTR gene.

Since the CF gene was found in 1989[3,4,5], huge strides have been made in understanding CF and its impact on so many parts of the body.

Why CFTR is so important

15

CF transmembrane conductance regulator (CFTR) protein acts as a channel through the outer layer of cells which lines many of the body's hollow tubes and tissues that produce mucus and fluids. These include the sweat glands, the airways, the pancreas, and parts of the reproductive organs.

CFTR protein controls the flow of electrically charged atoms of chlorine – called chloride ions – in and out of the epithelial cells. Chloride ions are important chemicals in the body and affect the amount of water going in and out of cells. Chloride combines with sodium to form sodium chloride – common salt.

We don't yet fully understand how CFTR protein works. But if there is a problem with it – as in CF – chloride transport is blocked. For example, sodium chloride may be left in the fluid that comes out of the sweat glands, making the sweat on the skin very salty. In fact, salty sweat is a hallmark of CF.

In contrast, in the lungs of people with CF, chloride gets trapped inside the cells, along with the fluid it should be escorting from the tissues into the airways. This reduces the amount of water in the airway mucus which, in turn, becomes thick, sticky, and difficult to clear from the lungs. Instead, it obstructs air passages and easily becomes infected.

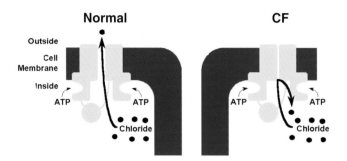

Fig 3. – *Chloride transport by CFTR: In normal cells, CFTR is activated by energy rich molecules of ATP (adenosine triphosphate) and allows chloride to pass out of cells through the cell membrane. In CF cells, CFTR malfunctions and blocks chloride transport.*

We need to know much more about the way transport of chloride and other ions is changed by defective CFTR protein. But it seems that the organs most affected by CF – the lungs, intestines, sweat glands, pancreas, and the male sperm-carrying tubes *(vas deferens)* – all need fully functioning CFTR protein in order to work normally.

CF: A Genetic Disorder

17

As CF is caused by a change in the structure of a gene, it is known as a genetic, or inherited, disorder

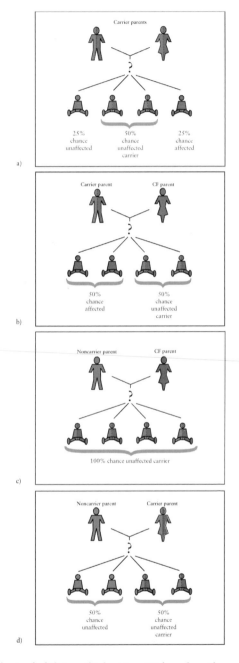

Fig 4. – Shows the probabilities of inheriting CF based on the genetic make-up of the parents. Inheritance probabilities when a) both parents are CF carriers; b) one parent is a CF carrier and one parent has CF; c) one parent has CF and one is a non-carrier; and d) one parent is a carrier and one is a non-carrier.

© SPInc 2000

which is passed from generation to generation
(see Figure 4).

Genes are pieces of DNA strung together on chromosomes – spiral structures found in the nucleus of
every cell. We all have 46 chromosomes, arranged
in 23 pairs. In each pair, one chromosome is
contributed by your mother, the other by your father.

The CFTR gene involved in CF is found on chromosome 7. As everyone has a pair of chromosome 7s,
they also have two copies of the CFTR gene.

The gene is 'recessive', which means that you need
to inherit two genes containing a mutation – one
from your mother and one from your father – to
have the symptoms of CF. Someone with only one
mutation will be a carrier who can pass on the gene
but will not have symptoms of the condition.

Almost 2.5 million people in the UK are carriers of
CF. If a couple who are both carriers decide to have
a child, there is a 1 in 4 chance in each pregnancy
of having a child with CF.

One Gene, Many Mutations

Over 900 different mutations of the CFTR gene have been found, and new mutations are still being discovered. Most are very rare. In fact, the 12 commonest mutations are responsible for over 90% of cases of CF.

The most frequent mutation among people of European descent is called delta F508, sometimes written as ΔF508. In people with this mutation, the CFTR channels are not made properly. They are not inserted into cell membranes where they need to be in order to function properly.

Other, less common mutations may produce CFTR channels that function better than those arising from the ΔF508 mutation.

As different CFTR gene mutations produce CFTR proteins with different levels of function, you might think that there would be a clear connection between the type of CFTR mutation and the severity of CF symptoms. But unfortunately it isn't like that!

There are a number of reasons why it is hard to predict how your CFTR mutations will affect you:

One person, two very different mutations

Everyone with CF has two CFTR genes – one inherited from their mother, the other from their father. But the mutations may be quite different, and different combinations of mutations can produce different patterns of disease. In fact there are so many possible combinations that it is impossible to predict the effects of every combination.

Dominant mutations

Some mutations dominate others, so one can cover up the effects of another. This can happen with some CFTR gene mutations that affect the need for pancreatic enzymes. If you inherit a mutation that enables you to produce functioning CFTR proteins in your pancreatic ducts, this may dominate a mutation that does not. So you may be able to produce your own pancreatic enzymes.

21

The ΔF508 mutation is closely linked to poor pancreatic function (pancreatic insufficiency) and, with the ΔF508 mutation so common in the UK, it is not surprising that 90% of people with CF in this country have pancreatic insufficiency[2].

Someone with two ΔF508 mutations is likely to need pancreatic supplements, but if there is only one ΔF508 mutation – or none at all – it is possible that the pancreas will still produce sufficient enzymes to digest the food. For example, two mutations – R117H and A455E – will over-ride the effects of a ΔF508 mutation and result in pancreatic sufficiency.

Organ sensitivity

Some parts of the body are more sensitive than others to defects in the CFTR protein – the pancreas is obviously one. Another is the *vas deferens* – the male reproductive tube that carries sperm from the testes to the penis. As this needs normal CFTR proteins in order to develop properly, over 95% of men with CF do not have *vas deferens*, and are therefore infertile. Indeed, in very mild forms of CF, infertility may be the only problem[6].

The severity of respiratory symptoms cannot currently be related directly to the type of CFTR gene mutation. Numerous external factors, including adherence to treatment, exposure to viral infections and cigarette smoke, nutrition, and social and economic factors have a major impact on the severity of respiratory symptoms, no matter which CFTR genes are present[7,8].

Overall genetic make-up and environment

Inheriting two copies of the ΔF508 mutation is generally associated with a poorer outlook than some other combinations of mutations. Yet every CF doctor knows patients with this genetic profile who do very well and, equally, other patients with less serious mutations who do less well.

No one knows exactly why this should be, but a variety of other genetic, psychosocial and environmental factors have been suggested. Our genes do not work in isolation. Genes on one chromosome can affect those on an entirely different chromosome. So it is quite possible that genes which appear to have no direct role in CF, do still have some impact – by adding to or offsetting the effects of CFTR mutations.

Although genes play a key role in how we develop physically and mentally, environmental factors also play a part. Just as exposure to viruses and cigarette smoke affect lung function in people with CF, so other environmental factors – including diet and nutrition – are likely to affect other aspects of the disease.

Neither genes alone nor environment tell the whole story.

Diagnosis of CF

If you are reading this book, you probably know that you have CF or you know someone who has the condition.

In some parts of the UK, CF is discovered as a result of routinely testing newborn babies. But, in most cases, CF is diagnosed on the basis of clinical signs and symptoms (Figure 2, page 15). An abnormal amount of chloride in the sweat, a chronic, productive cough, frequent chest infections, clubbed fingers and digestive problems are typical symptoms[9]. In some cases, fertility problems may lead to a diagnosis of CF.

The standard test to confirm the diagnosis of CF is the sweat test. Pilocarpine, a drug that makes you sweat, is drawn painlessly through the skin with a small electric current. Sweat is absorbed onto filter paper and analysed for sodium and chloride content. A value less than 40mmol/L is definitely normal, while a figure above 60mmol/L is considered positive. However, a result between 40 and 60mmol/L is borderline and, as sweat tests can be abnormal for other reasons, will require further investigation.

If possible, the sweat test should be performed at a laboratory used to carrying out the test as it can be difficult to perform correctly and, as explained

above, the results may be hard to interpret. The
test is performed twice to be sure that the results
are accurate.

Genetic testing may also be done to confirm the
diagnosis and/or identify the mutations. A simple
mouthwash sample provides cells which are checked
for DNA sequences that correspond to CF gene
mutations. Although there are so many mutations,
some are much more common than others, and
routine testing methods should detect about 85%
of them.

Screening for CF carriers

CFTR gene mutations are common in the UK. One
in 25 people are carriers and most have no idea they
could have an affected child. CF carrier screening
is not offered routinely in the UK; only relatives of
CF families who are at higher than average risk are
likely to be offered a genetic test. (Sweat tests are
not abnormal in CF carriers).

Since routine antenatal screening could detect and

inform almost three quarters of high risk couples, the CF Trust feels that health authorities should now consider offering them this choice.

For example, screening could be available at GPs' surgeries and at antenatal clinics. The Trust has carried out pilot projects which have demonstrated the practical and economic feasibility of such schemes.

Although CF affects many parts of the body, most everyday problems are about breathing and digestion. The aim of everyday care – medication, physiotherapy, exercise and nutrition – is to keep lung and digestive function as good as possible, so the likelihood of complications is reduced.

Living with any serious, long term medical condition can also put a strain on how you feel emotionally – and CF is no exception. No one should feel embarrassed about getting anxious or depressed if things aren't going well. Sorting out the emotional ups and downs of everyday life with CF is just as important as attending to the physical problems.

Breathing difficulties

CF affects all of the airways, from the nose and sinuses, right down into the lungs. Most people with CF cough up mucus, wheeze or have trouble breathing. Blocked or runny nose, sinus pain and headaches are also common symptoms.

The frequent coughing in CF can be very embarrassing. You've probably watched as shoppers and commuters back away in case they catch your dreadful disease. They glare as if to say 'can't you do something about that?' Well, of course you can't, but you may not want to announce the reason for your cough to every passer-by. Everyone deals with such situations in their own way, but it may help to talk about your feelings with someone in your CF team or with others experiencing the same problem.

BOX 1
Know me by my name, not my disease
Anon

I cannot remember a time when I had no cough, but I have only become conscious of it and the effects on others and the attention it draws to me since I reached adulthood and no longer live in the shadow of a protective mother.

During my teenage years I never kept my CF a secret and, as I lived in a small community and couldn't exactly be classed as a 'young lady' I never saw it as a problem. A day wouldn't pass without me breaking wind on several occasions amidst the daily dirty joke and, when under the influence of alcohol, I often circulated 'my friend, the phlob pot' for donations! Although the neighbours liked to think of me as the 'poor little sick girl', I was not that sick and no longer very little.

29

I am now in my late 20s and my lifestyle is far more sedate. I thoroughly enjoyed my wild child years, but it's not what I want now. I'm quite content to sit in front of the fire with my life-time partner and our dog and watch TV of an evening.

Denial was never an issue for me . . . . . until now. Denial and suppression go hand in hand as, outside the home, I try to salvage what I have left of the right to choose how much people know about my life with CF. I suppress laughter to avoid breathless gasps of coughing and I try not to cough at all, wherever I am. Now, I resent everyone wanting to know my business. I twist an innocent 'How are you?' into 'How are you coping?' although much of the time it's a correct interpretation.

I've found that to answer 'I'm fine, how are you?' soon shows whether it was a casual question or they are determined to probe information I don't want to reveal. Now, I need to escape these probing questions however sincere they may be. If you'd told me 10 years ago that I'd be taking detours to avoid people I know or pretending not to see them, I wouldn't have believed you. But now it happens all the time!

Lung damage

The lungs become damaged because people with CF can't clear all the mucus from their airways (see Figure 5).

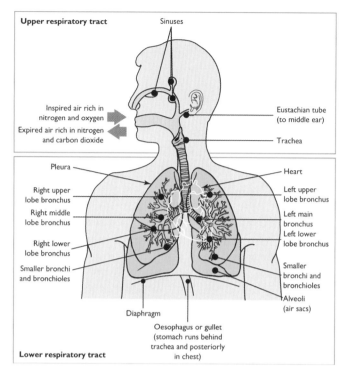

Fig 5. – The airways and gas exchange. Each lung contains a branching network of fine tubes, or airways. The small airways (bronchioles) lead to even smaller airways (alveolar ducts) and finally to air sacs (alveoli). Oxygen – from the air you breathe in – goes through the walls of the air sacs into the bloodstream and, in return, carbon dioxide passes back from the blood into the air sacs, ready to be breathed out.

From Cystic Fibrosis: The Facts by Ann Harris and Maurice Super (3rd edition, 1995) © Ann Harris and Maurice Super 1995.

Mucus is produced by cells in the airway lining to defend the lungs from attack by bacteria, viruses and other airborne invaders. Normally, it is watery and free-flowing and kept moving by tiny hairs, called cilia, attached to the surface of the airway cells. As these hairs beat back and forth, any foreign particles trapped in the mucus, are pushed up the airways and eventually coughed up, or swallowed down into the stomach.

In CF this doesn't happen. The mucus is thick because the CFTR protein does not transport chloride ions effectively, and the cilia themselves may be faulty.

Whatever the reason, the difficulty in clearing mucus from the airways seems to set the stage for a continuous cycle of infection and inflammation (Figure 6).

Inflammation or infection?

Infection often occurs very early in life and it seems likely that the infected mucus, which is 'trapped' in the airways, triggers the inflammation.

Inflammation is the body's normal reaction to injury caused by an irritant (such as a plug of mucus) or a microbe (such as a bacterium). A variety of white

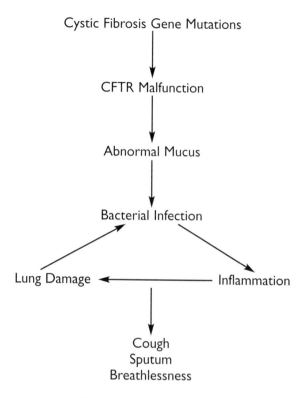

Fig 6. – CF Gene Mutation. Inflammation or infection?

blood cells rush to the trouble zone and release enzymes and other substances to destroy the intruder. In doing so, they make the surrounding area temporarily inflamed and swollen.

In CF, this inflammation can become permanent and gradually damages the fragile airways, making them susceptible to infection.

33

Bacterial and fungal infection

When someone with CF gets a bacterial lung infection for the first time, *Staphylococcus aureus* is usually to blame. At this stage, it can usually be eradicated, but regular sputum tests will be needed to check for any sign of a return, especially if there is a change in the amount or colour of the sputum.

In adults with CF, *Pseudomonas aeruginosa* is likely to be more of a problem. According to data from the European Registry for CF, two thirds of people with CF in the UK have *P. aeruginosa*, while just under 10% have *S. aureus*[10].

The first time that Pseudomonas infection occurs, every effort should be made to get rid of all bacteria. This means a course of an inhaled antibiotic and either an oral or IV antibiotic. Research has shown that this approach can keep Pseudomonas at bay for a number of years[11]. When it does come back, a repeat approach can often get rid of the bacterium for another year or more.

Unfortunately, repeated infection eventually makes it

very difficult to get rid of Pseudomonas, and long term treatment is geared to keeping it under control rather than eradicating it completely.

Nearly all people with CF eventually become infected with Pseudomonas, but the longer this can be delayed the better the outcome. An increasing number of UK centres recognise the need for prevention and control of pseudomonal cross-infection and hold separate clinics for individuals with different profiles of infection.

In the last few years, other lung infections have become a problem for people with CF. These include *Burkholderia cepacia* (formerly known as *Pseudomonas cepacia*). Data from the European Registry suggest that about 1 in 14 people with CF in the UK are infected with *B. cepacia*[10].

This organism does not usually cause infection in healthy people, but it results in serious and rapid lung damage in some people with CF[12]. Those who already have poor lung function are particularly at risk. So it is very important to prevent *B. cepacia* from spreading.

35

Some strains of *B. cepacia* may be more easily transmitted than others, but the bacterium can be spread by droplet infection when people meet, through equipment used to treat CF or during physiotherapy sessions.

Because *B. cepacia* can be spread by person-to-person contact, CF centres separate patients who are infected with the bacterium from those who are not. The CF Trust recommends that everyone with CF should be tested for *B. cepacia*, and that anyone who is infected should not mix with other people with CF, at meetings or socially[12]. Even mixing with other infected individuals may be hazardous as it is possible to pick up a more serious strain of the bacterium.

The CF Trust recommends a number of simple hygiene precautions to prevent the spread of all infections, including *B. cepacia* (Box 2, page 37).

Finding that you have *B. cepacia* can be a lonely and depressing time. Keeping away from other people with CF makes medical sense but can be very isolating. Discussing your feelings with your medical team or with people in the same situation – by phone, e-mail or good old fashioned letter – can help break down some of the barriers.

B. cepacia infection is difficult to treat, but sometimes the bacterium can be cleared from the sputum. People who have at least three negative sputum tests, spread over 12 months, are considered to be free from infection.

BOX 2
Avoiding infection through good hygiene

- Always cover your mouth and nose when you cough or sneeze
- Wash your hands frequently, particularly if you cough a lot
- When using toilet/bathroom facilities, avoid ordinary multi-use soap bars and opt for anti-bacterial dispenser soap, disposable paper towels or hot air hand dryers
- Do not leave sputum pots uncovered
- Throw tissues away immediately after you use them
- Do not share physiotherapy equipment such as nebulisers or frames
- Do not eat or drink using the same utensils as others
- Do not share drink cans, cups or bottles
- Refrain from shaking hands with others. An alternative friendly gesture might be a gentle touch of the arm or shoulder
- Use single rooms in the event of requiring overnight accommodation and avoid visiting other people's rooms

Other bacteria, including *Stenotrophomonas maltophilia* (previously called *Xanthomonas maltophilia*), *Alkaligines xylosoxidans*, or methi-cillin-resistant *S. aureus* (MRSA) also cause respiratory tract infections in people with CF. Treatment may not be straightforward as some strains have become resistant to some common antibiotics.

In recent years, fungi, such as Aspergillus, have been recognised as important causes of lung problems in adults with CF.

Aspergillus can trigger an allergic reaction which produces symptoms like those of CF and asthma. As in CF, the inflammation which results may lead to permanent lung damage. Aspergillus can complicate the underlying lung disease in CF, so it's important to diagnose and treat it early. People with CF should avoid spending long periods in damp rooms which contain organic material such as hay.

The need to measure lung function

Measuring lung function is an important aspect of

assessing your CF, and it is helpful in deciding the need for and response to treatment. However, measurements should be interpreted in the light of previous results and other aspects of your disease, such as symptoms and body weight.

Nearly all lung function tests measure the flow of air into and out of the lungs. The commonest tests are FEV_1 (forced expiratory volume in one second) and FVC (forced vital capacity). In most clinics this is checked at every visit (usually two or three monthly – see CF Trust's Patient's Charter[13]).

FEV_1 measures the amount of air you can blow out of your lungs in one second. FVC (forced vital capacity) is the total amount of air you can breathe out after taking the largest breath you can. It provides additional information about the state of your lungs.

All adults with CF should have these tests done routinely each time they go to the clinic (see reference to the CF Trust's Patient's Charter on page 105, setting out the essential healthcare that people with CF should expect to receive).

The health of your lungs is assessed according to how closely your FEV_1 compares with that of someone of the same age who does not have CF. In general, lung function deteriorates with age (Table 1) but people vary in how quickly this happens. If chronic infection can be avoided, lung function may remain stable for years.

Table 1. – *Classification of lung disease severity (these values give a rough guide to the degree of lung damage due to CF but form only a part of the CF assessment)*

Mild	FEV_1 70%–90% of expected result
Moderate	FEV_1 40%–69% of expected result
Severe	FEV_1 less than 40% of predicted result

© SPInc 2000

Everyday care of lung function

Most serious CF complications and deaths are related to lung disease, so everyday activities that maintain or improve your lung function are very important. These include physiotherapy, exercise and medication.

Daily physiotherapy is the foundation stone of lung

care in CF, and many techniques are available[14]. These are briefly described in Table 2. You will probably be advised to do your physiotherapy for at least 15 minutes per day, but the choice of technique (or combination of techniques) is based on the severity of your lung disease, your living arrangements, and what you are most likely to use regularly. Your CF team can help you decide which physiotherapy technique best suits your needs, and

Table 2

© SPInc 2000

Physiotherapy Techniques for People With CF	
Technique	**Description**
Active Cycle of Breathing (ACBT)	Loosens secretions and keeps the chest mobile through breathing control, deep breathing and huffing
Autogenic Drainage	Uses controlled breathing at different levels of the lungs. Each breath consists of a slow gentle breath in, a breath hold for three seconds and a fast breath out
Positive Expiratory Pressure (PEP)	Uses a device (with face mask) to provide resistance to breathing out. This helps keep small airways open and loosen secretions
High Pressure PEP	Also uses a mask, like PEP, but with differences in breathing technique and higher pressures
Oscillating PEP (Flutter Therapy)	Hand-held device produces a vibrator effect to the airways during breathing out
Postural Drainage	Mainly used in infants, it uses gravity to assist drainage during percussion and breathing exercises
High Frequency Chest Wall Oscillation	Rarely available in the UK, an inflatable vest compresses the chest wall at set frequencies during huffing

41

a physiotherapist who specialises in CF should teach you how to do it effectively.

Exercise is also important, and many adults enjoy cycling, swimming, running and walking. Exercise mobilises mucus prior to physiotherapy, and better clearance of secretions can increase your resistance to infection. Even a day on the rides at a theme park can help mobilise sputum!

However, exercise alone is no substitute for physio-therapy. Some people with severe lung disease may be able to exercise with the help of extra oxygen – something they need to talk to their doctor or physiotherapist about.

Many people with CF also use one or more medications. Most are breathed directly into the lungs by inhaler or nebuliser. Inhaled broncho-dilators such as beta-agonists (e.g. Ventolin and Bricanyl) and theophylline widen the airways to make it easier to breathe in and out. Inhaled anti-inflammatory agents such as corticosteroids (e.g. Pulmicort and Flixotide) reduce inflammation in the airways, and mucolytic agents make the mucus in the lungs thinner and easier to cough up.

DNase (Pulmozyme) thins mucus and breaks it down so it can be cleared more effectively with physiotherapy. It improves lung function in some people with CF who have mild or moderate lung disease (see Table 1, page 40). It also has some benefit in those with severe disease, but it is not always easy to predict who will get the most out of DNase.

The benefits of regular maintenance IV antibiotic treatment for Pseudomonas infection during periods of good health have not been firmly established[15]. In some CF units, preventive treatment with IV antibiotics, given every 3 months, has proved helpful[16]. Unfortunately, few oral antibiotics are effective against *P. aeruginosa*, and prolonged use of these few drugs make some strains of Pseudomonas resistant to these antibiotics.

Nebulised colistin (Colomycin) has been widely used in the last decade both to treat early Pseudomonas infection and to suppress chronic infection. Recently, a preservative-free formulation of tobramycin

43

(TOBI) – an antibiotic used intravenously – has become available for nebulisation. Results of trials in the USA have shown that treatment with TOBI can maintain or improve lung function in people with CF, particularly teenagers[17]. UK doctors are currently assessing how the new tobramycin formulation should be used here.

In clinical trials, some children with mild CF have benefited from preventive treatment with high dose ibuprofen, an anti-inflammatory agent[18]. Treatment appeared to slow deterioration in lung function. But doctors are concerned that long term use of such large doses of ibuprofen could damage the lining of the stomach, and there are doubts over the value of therapy in adults. So research is continuing.

Digestive problems

CF affects the digestive system in many ways, but the most important and almost invariable effect is on the pancreas. The pancreas is an organ which lies behind the stomach (Figure 7). It has a long head and a tapering tail, and is about 15cm long.

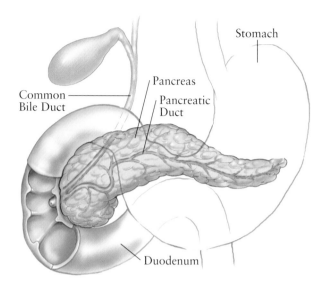

Stomach

Pancreas

Common
Bile Duct

Pancreatic
Duct

Duodenum

Fig 7. – The pancreas is near the duodenum, the section of the small intestine closest to the stomach.   © SPInc 2000

It has two main functions: enzyme secretion (exocrine) and hormone production (endocrine) e.g. insulin.

Normally the pancreas secretes juice containing digestive enzymes. The main enzymes, lipase, amylase and protease, break down fat, carbo-hydrates and protein into small absorbable components. The pancreatic juice travels along fine tubes in the pancreas, called ducts, and are then released into the small intestine, where most food is digested. Pancreatic juice is an alkaline fluid, like that produced by mixing bicarbonate of soda with water. This fluid neutralises the stomach acid that accompanies the partially digested nutrients that enter the small intestine from the stomach.

The endocrine tissue in the pancreas consists of tiny spherical "islets of Langerhans", which secrete insulin and glucagon (hormones which help to control the blood sugar levels). The islets only make up less than 1% of the pancreas, and most of the pancreas is dedicated to the exocrine function.

In people with CF, there is a build up of thick fluid in the pancreatic ducts, owing to a lack of CFTR protein. This blocks and damages the ducts, leading to reduced production of digestive enzymes ('pancreatic insufficiency'). In addition, the pancreatic fluid which people with CF make isn't alkaline enough to neutralise the stomach acid properly.

In the UK, this pancreatic enzyme insufficiency affects more than 9 out of 10 people with CF. In the 1994 CF adult survey, only about 6% of respondents did not need pancreatic enzymes[2]. Without pancreatic enzymes, fats, proteins and carbohydrates aren't properly digested and absorbed. The large, bulky stools containing much undigested fat (steatorrhoea), which are a common early symptom of CF, are a direct result of the lack of pancreatic enzymes.

Pancreatic enzyme insufficiency is treated with pancreatic enzyme supplements, which should be taken with fat-containing meals or snacks, including milk[19].

Pancreatic Enzyme Supplements

Most people with CF need pancreatic enzyme supplements to replace the enzymes usually produced by the pancreas so that they can digest and absorb fats and proteins properly. The more fat in a meal, the more enzymes they need. The dose should be varied depending on the fat content of the meal, snack or drink.

Not all pancreatic enzymes are the same. They are available in different strengths, ranging from 5000 to 25,000 units of lipase (enzymes that digest fat) per capsule. Capsules come in different sizes too. The granules inside the capsules of many brands are 'enteric-coated' to prevent them from being dissolved in the acidic juices of the stomach.

This enteric coating is designed to break down and release enzyme particles in the duodenum – the first part of the small intestine where food is digested. The duodenum is less acidic than the stomach, but, if the pancreatic fluid is low in bicarbonate and does not neutralise the acid entering the duodenum from the stomach, the enteric-coated capsules may not dissolve properly. A few people may need to take drugs, such as proton pump inhibitors (e.g. Losec) to reduce the amount of stomach acid.

Other health problems, including infections, coeliac or Crohn's disease, and liver disease, can also affect fat and protein absorption. So be sure to check with your doctor or dietitian at your CF centre before adjusting your dose of enzymes, as you may need some tests.

A change in eating habits can also affect the activity of your enzymes, and it's important to take appropriate amounts of enzymes for different meals and snacks.

Finally, make sure that your enzyme supply has not passed its expiry date or been damaged by heat or dampness.

Fibrosing colonopathy

In the early 1990s, a rare bowel disorder called fibrosing colonopathy was reported in a small number of children with CF taking large doses of both high- and low-strength pancreatic enzymes. Fibrosing colonopathy has been associated with some formulations of enzymes but not with others. More specifically, it is likely that an important factor in causing fibrosing colonopathy is the methacrylic acid copolymer (Eudragit) used in some enteric coatings[20]. The leaflet in the pack of enzymes should specify all the ingredients.

The UK government's advisory group – the Committee on Safety of Medicines – has issued the following recommendations[21]:

- Pancrease HL and Nutrizym 22 should not be used in children with CF aged 15 or less (Creon 25,000 has thus far not been associated with fibrosing colonopathy)
- The total dose of supplementary pancreatic enzyme should not exceed 10,000 lipase units/kg daily.

Since 1994, there have been no new cases of fibrosing colonopathy in the UK. It may be the dose of the enteric coating, not the dose of the enzyme itself which is responsible for causing this disorder[22]. If you are concerned about abdominal symptoms or the dose or brand of your enzymes, this should be discussed with your clinic doctor.

Good nutrition

Eating properly is essential for people with CF. Pancreatic enzyme supplements improve fat and protein absorption, but you need to eat plenty of high-energy foods for the enzymes to work on.

This advice may seem at odds with current healthy eating guidance to the population in general. But if you have CF your energy requirements are much greater than those of other people because of the extra effort you put into breathing. So there is no doubt that a high energy diet is the answer.

Generally, people with CF have no restrictions on food, and they should eat a healthy, balanced diet. But it is important to discuss this aspect of your care with your doctor and dietitian.

Most people need vitamin supplements because they may not absorb fat-soluble vitamins, particularly vitamins A, D and E, properly. A lack of vitamins causes a number of problems, for example, with eyesight and increased risk of infection. The usual recommendation for vitamin supplementation is a multivitamin supplement that contains vitamin A (8000 IU), vitamin D (800 IU) and vitamin E (200 mg). However, doses should be adjusted to individual requirements, according to the results of annual blood tests.

Most CF units check vitamin levels and carry out various blood tests as part of the annual review.

An exacerbation, or worsening, of lung disease is
the most common reason why the everyday care
of CF gets disrupted. It's usually due to a new or
worsening infection and the outward signs of
increased breathing problems are quite obvious.
Some people accept that exacerbations are an
unwanted aspect of their CF. But they can still be
very distressing. They disrupt your normal working
and social life. They upset your family and those
who care about you. Holidays may have to be
cancelled, outings postponed. There's disappoint-
ment all around.

During an exacerbation, you may feel pretty low.
In addition to feeling physically tired and unwell
now, there's the possibility that your health
may continue to decline. Are your exacerbations
getting more frequent? Will you keep needing
to go into hospital or have courses of IV antibiotics?
When will you be able to get back to your normal
routine?

These and lots of other questions are bound to go
buzzing around your head. Maybe you feel able

to talk about them with your family or friends, maybe you don't. They're probably having the same thoughts but they may also find it difficult to talk about them in case they upset you.

This sort of uncertainty, confusion and lack of communication is the perfect breeding ground for anxiety and depression. Anyone can be optimistic when they feel great; it's much harder to look on the bright side when you're feeling ill.

It's easy to say, much harder to do, but there's nothing like talking about your worries. It won't make them go away overnight, nor will it make your physical symptoms clear up. But it will help you see the wood for the trees. It'll help you realise some of your worries are unnecessary, some have practical solutions, and some just can't be solved.

Who you talk to will depend on you, your family and friends, and the 'talking services' which your CF team or your GP can provide (see page 98).

Treating breathing problems

Since exacerbations are usually due to a new or worsening infection, the treatment of breathing problems is based on antibiotics and improved airway clearance. The CF Trust has recently published guidelines on use of antibiotics in the treatment of CF (report of the UK CF Trust Antibiotic Group – April 2000)[23].

Recognizing the signs and symptoms of these episodes is crucial because stepped-up treatment at home or in hospital is necessary to prevent additional problems. Sixty per cent of those who took part in the 1994 CF adults survey had been admitted to hospital in the previous year[2]. There were an average 1.7 admissions and the same number of courses of home IV treatment per person per year.

The early warning signs of an exacerbation are:
• Increased cough
• Increased sputum production and/or a change in appearance of sputum
• Fever
• Reduced appetite

- Weight loss
- Time off college or work (due to illness) in the previous week
- Increased breathing rate and/or difficulty breathing
- New findings on chest examination (eg: wheezing, crackles)
- Reduced ability to exercise
- Decrease in FEV_1 from usual levels, of 10% or more within past 3 months
- Decrease in the amount of oxygen in the blood (haemoglobin saturation) of 5% or more compared with usual levels in the previous 3 months
- New finding(s) on chest x-ray.

Treatment for an exacerbation affecting the lungs usually takes 14 days, but may take longer, depending on symptoms and the rate of improvement. More intensive physiotherapy will mobilise secretions and get infected mucus out of the lungs. Intravenous antibiotic therapy is often needed.

The choice of antibiotics depends on the results of your most recent sputum culture and antibiotic sensitivity tests. These may need to be repeated because adults with CF may be infected with more

than one strain of bacterium or even multiple species
of Pseudomonas, some of which may be resistant
to several antibiotics.

Using combinations of antibiotics reduces the risk
of resistance. Infections caused by *P. aeruginosa*
are often treated with combinations of an amino-
glycoside (eg: tobramycin, gentamicin, amikacin)
and an anti-pseudomonal beta-lactam (ceftazidime,
azlocillin, tazobactam, meropenem, aztreonam) or
a quinolone (generally ciprofloxacin). Resistant
strains of *P. aeruginosa* are sometimes treated with
intravenous colistin.

Exacerbations can be treated in hospital or at home,
depending on their severity and the availability of
help at home. Some people prefer home treatment
because it is less disruptive to their normal routine,
while others find it a burden[23,24].

People who do opt for home treatment need to have
good IV access, and they need to be well trained and
confident in what they are doing. They also need
careful monitoring and will need check ups at
the CF units during treatment and afterwards.

Nutritional support

When you have an exacerbation, your body
needs more energy to deal with the extra effort of
breathing and fight infection. But you may not feel
well enough to eat. Nutritional supplements, which
concentrate nutrients into small amounts of liquid
can help to boost your calorie intake when you
don't feel like eating. There are many types available
– ask your dietitian for more information.

If nutrition is a continuing problem, tube feeding
of food supplements may be the answer. There
are several kinds of tube; a nasogastric tube goes
through the nose into the oesophagus and down
into the stomach and can be used at night for short
periods. But it may be uncomfortable if you are
coughing a lot.

More permanent tubes, which are inserted through
the abdominal wall, directly into the stomach or
small intestine, are a better option for longer-term
treatment. These are called percutaneous endo-
scopically-placed gastrostomy tubes (PEGs).
Recent improvements in design have improved

their comfort and convenience and you can still eat as well! The tube can be replaced with a button, a device which sits flat against the stomach wall. About 5–10% of adults with CF have gastrostomies.

Daily Care:
Who Has Time to Do It All?

The daily care of CF is time-consuming. The physiotherapy sessions, the exercise sessions, the medications, the preparation and consumption of a well-balanced diet – who has time to do it all? How does the routine fit in with work or college or family responsibilities?

If you have difficulty squeezing it all into a day, you're not alone. A survey of 60 adults with CF carried out a few years ago in the UK showed that almost 70% of the study participants failed to do their physiotherapy as prescribed[25]. Three quarters exercised regularly and most people took enzymes with every meal. But only 25% always used enzymes with snacks and about half took vitamins on a regular basis.

As you might expect, aspects of treatment that produced immediate benefits were done more frequently. Study participants who felt that physiotherapy or exercise sessions improved their breathing tended to do them more regularly.

Compliance With Physiotherapy

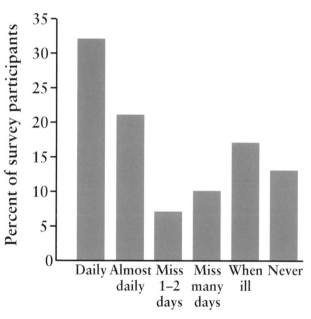

Fig 8. – Adherence With Physiotherapy. Proportion of survey participants (60 adults with CF) performing physiotherapy at various intervals[25].　© SPInc 2000

Being aware of the importance of sticking to your treatment regime doesn't mean you'll actually do it.

Research has shown that there is a gap between perceived and real understanding of techniques. Even well informed people have misconceptions and their knowledge needs regular updates.

For others, failing to carry out their treatment is their way of showing that this is one part of their life where they are in charge. Just as some people with eating disorders use food as their weapon against authority, others use their ability to reject treatment as their way to get back at their disease and all the limitations it tries to put in their way.

Finally, some people with CF make full-informed choices about which aspects of their treatment they will do and which they will miss out. They trade the benefit that a particular treatment might give to their health against the drawbacks it has for their everyday life.

Clearly, there is no simple answer which will suit everyone. But negotiating an acceptable treatment regime with the CF team – with doctor, physiotherapist, dietitian, nurse, etc, all fully aware of how long each component of care can take you –

is a better solution than pretending that you're doing everything you've been told.

Being open with your CF team will help you to find a compromise solution – a package of treatment which will fit in better with your lifestyle requirements but won't leave your doctor and therapists wanting to strangle you.

BOX 3
Finding time for treatment
Teresa Jacklin

I used to be terrible at doing my physiotherapy. But at that time my chest was completely unproductive, so I could afford to be.

Eventually, thanks to an open relationship with my doctor, I admitted the truth. After all, I explained, what was the point of making myself feel ill from all that coughing when there was nothing in my chest to cough up?

At the age of 24 I caught Pseudomonas and was prescribed a colistin nebuliser to suppress the infection. As this made perfect sense to me, I complied. It takes 15 minutes twice a day, but you can do other things, such as write or apply make-up at the same time. The lipstick has to go on last for obvious reasons.

I continued to have clear lungs which I believe was at least partly due to the colistin. But I still had problems doing my physiotherapy, even when I needed it during exacerbations, because I had developed arthritis and tipping on a wedge was painful.

Thankfully, the physiotherapist at my new hospital has been more than happy to listen to my specific problems and has taught me to use the Active Cycle of Breathing technique, which works brilliantly for me. She is also ordering me a flutter, which I will be able to use while I'm doing something else.

But combined with my joint exercises, I need over 1.5 hours per day to do my physiotherapy and at least 30 minutes for my nebuliser. I must admit I can't always find the time. But when I do, and when I succeed, I don't have a cough for the rest of the day.

I honestly believe that the 100% compliant patient, who does everything that they are supposed to do, every single day, is as mythical as the Holy Grail.

Many people I have spoken to say that they only do treatments when there is a clear and direct benefit. Nebulising salbutamol gets done as it eases breathing straight away, whereas colistin gets neglected because the benefits of taking it are long term. I feel that we need to discuss the demands of our treatment regimes with our care team. Your doctor can help to identify which components are beneficial to you and the specific characteristics of each treatment, for example colistin needs to be taken consistently and DNase needs to be followed with physiotherapy. That way when real life gets in the way and you need to cut corners with your treatment, you can make sure it's a corner that has least impact on your health.

Everyone becomes more prone to illness as they get older, whether or not they have CF. Heart disease, cancer, diabetes and arthritis are just a few of the conditions which become more common as we get older.

Adults with CF get some of these age-related problems as well as those due to the progressive damage related specifically to their CF. It's not surprising therefore that, although many adults stay very well, they do tend to get more complications than children with CF.

Physical complications can be divided broadly into three categories – affecting the lungs, the digestive system, and the bones and joints. As with exacerbations, the development of CF complications can make people feel anxious and depressed, angry or upset.

Teenagers and young adults with CF will be contending with the emotional highs and lows of increasing independence, further education, getting a job and making new relationships, and the additional hassle and frustration of becoming more responsible for their everyday care. Small wonder that, when things are going badly, they may question whether it's all worth the effort.

Respiratory complications

You've already read about the impact of chest infections and exacerbations. But adults with CF are also prone to a range of more or less common complications affecting their airways. These include sinusitis and minor bleeding from the lungs (which is quite common), and rarely more severe bleeds, collapsed lung, and respiratory failure which need more intensive treatment.

Haemoptysis

Minor bleeding from blood vessels in the lungs is quite common, and you'll see streaks of blood in your sputum. Usually, no special treatment is needed, but you should go to your doctor if this persists, as you may be having an exacerbation

which requires antibiotics or other therapy (see
If You Have An Exacerbation, page 52).

Major bleeds are rare and affect only about 2%
of adults with CF per year. In a major bleeding
episode, a cup (250 mls) or more of blood is lost
in a single day, or 100 mls per day are lost over
3 to 7 days. The bleeding usually comes from the
bronchial arteries that supply blood to the large
airways. These arteries often become expanded and
twisted as lung damage progresses.

Such bleeding almost always stops on its own in
a few days but, as it's likely to be due to an
exacerbation, antibiotics and other treatment will
probably be needed. Any drugs which can interfere
with blood clotting will usually be stopped. These
include common over-the-counter medicines such
as aspirin and other anti-inflammatory agents
(e.g. ibuprofen, naproxen sodium), as well as certain
antibiotics. So be sure to tell your doctor about all
the medicines you are taking, including those you
have bought at the chemist.

65

You'll need to discuss your physiotherapy routine with

your doctor and/or physiotherapist. Coughing up blood during physiotherapy may help breathing, but the active coughing may also lead to more bleeding.

In emergencies, a number of treatments may be used to stop bleeding. These include drugs, such as intravenous conjugated oestrogens, vasopressin, or desmopressin, and a blood transfusion is sometimes needed. Occasionally, it is necessary to make a blood clot form in the blood vessel in order to seal off the damaged area. This can be done by passing a tiny metal coil into the vessel, so blood cells will clot around it and stop the bleeding. Such procedures are done under local anaesthetic, via a small tube, or catheter, inserted into a blood vessel in your groin.

Although a major bleeding episode may be frightening, it does not necessarily mean that your health is getting worse. Your CF specialist will be able to assess the situation and discuss it with you.

Pneumothorax

This is a build up of air between the protective

layers of tissue (membranes called the pleura) which surround the lung. In adults with CF, it may arise because plugs of mucus prevent the air from being breathed out in the normal way. The resultant build-up of air within the chest cavity can put pressure on the lung and make it collapse.

Each year, pneumothorax occurs in about 2% of adults with CF, and about 1 in 5 will have a pneumothorax at some time in their life.

A small pneumothorax, in which only a small part of the lung collapses, may not cause any symptoms. Symptoms of a larger pneumothorax include sudden chest pain, increased heart rate, rapid breathing, shortness of breath, loss of colour in the face, and blueness around the lips or nail beds (cyanosis).

A small pneumothorax may get better on its own but you'll still need to go into hospital for 24 hours to make sure that all's well. A larger pneumothorax or one that causes symptoms usually needs to be drained. This involves putting a tube through the skin in the side of the chest under local anaesthetic and using a pump to suck out the air.

67

It's unwise to put any strain on a pneumothorax for at least 2 weeks after it has healed. Travel by air should not be undertaken for 4–6 weeks, and lung function tests are not usually performed during this time.

Sinusitis

Inflammation and swelling of the air cavities (sinuses) around the bridge of the nose is a common respiratory complication of CF. The condition usually begins in childhood, and may persist into adult life, often resulting in the formation of polyps – benign swellings which arise when the lining of the sinus drops into the nasal cavity.

The nose may be painfully congested and blocked, and the fluid which builds up in the nose and sinuses may become infected with Pseudomonas. Bacteria can then spread into the lungs.

Sinusitis and nasal polyps are sometimes diagnosed using fibre-optics, as this makes the nasal passages easier to see. A flexible viewing instrument (fibre-optic rhinoscope) is put up through the nostrils, and polyps can be removed or the nasal passages washed out. Recurrent problems may require sinus surgery to reduce the frequency of respiratory exacerbations.

Respiratory failure

When the lungs are damaged by inflammation and infection – as happens in CF – exchange of oxygen and carbon dioxide in the small air sacs of the lungs becomes inefficient. As a result, the amount of oxygen in the blood falls (hypoxaemia) and the level of carbon dioxide rises (hypercapnoea). This imbalance occurs in respiratory failure.

In people with CF, respiratory failure may accompany severe lung disease (usually indicated by an FEV_1 that is less than 25% of the expected value). It may also occur during a severe respiratory exacerbation in those with only moderate lung disease.

Breathing becomes difficult (dyspnoea) during activity and, in severe cases, at rest. Respiratory failure may also lead to heart and circulatory problems. Pulmonary hypertension – increased blood pressure in the blood vessels of the lungs – and cor pulmonale – an enlargement of the chamber (ventricle) on the right side of the heart – make it harder for the heart to deliver blood to the lungs. This further reduces the delivery of oxygen and removal of carbon dioxide.

Aggressive treatment

When respiratory failure first occurs, it is usually treated very aggressively because this can prevent complications from developing. The goal is to correct the imbalance in oxygen and carbon dioxide exchange.

This means intensifying your daily regimen – more physiotherapy, intravenous antibiotics to treat infection, anti-inflammatory agents, and enhanced nutrition. Exercise may also be useful in improving your ability to move air in and out of your lungs and to clear secretions.

If the first approach to treatment does not increase

blood oxygen content sufficiently, you may need supplementary oxygen. The dose is tailored to your requirements. Continuous therapy is recommended, although some people may only need oxygen at night.

Nasal intermittent ventilation (NIV) delivers oxygen through a mask. A ventilator sends oxygen into the mask under pressure, so this reduces the amount of effort you need to put into breathing. This approach can help you sleep better, as well as improving the amounts of oxygen and carbon dioxide in your blood and helping your lung function.

Mechanical ventilation may be used for short periods in people with CF when they are under-going specialist treatment in an intensive care unit, for example after a transplant. But it isn't very helpful in the treatment of advanced, long term respiratory failure.

Lung transplantation

Getting onto a transplant list is good news and bad

news. It's good news that there is another option for treatment. But it's also confirmation that time is running out. It's easy to talk positively and enthusiastically about lung transplants when you don't need one, much harder to stay cheerful when you're waiting for an organ.

Lung transplantation is a valuable option for some people with respiratory failure, and adults who have the operation generally do quite well, with up to half surviving five years or more[26].

People with *Burkholderia cepacia* infection may do less well after transplantation than uninfected individuals, and some transplant units do not normally operate on those with *B. cepacia*.

In general, women with CF and those who are 18 years of age or younger are likely to be considered for lung transplantation at an earlier stage of disease than others because their condition is known to progress faster.

But deciding to go on the list is a big step. It means accepting that you have reached a stage in your illness which requires an intervention generally seen as a last resort. It means that another boundary has been crossed – one that won't fit in with what you had planned for your life.

Few people make the decision to have a transplant without a lot of thought and discussion – with their family, their friends and their CF team. They naturally want to know what to expect before, during and after the operation. Some decide against surgery. Instead, they prefer to concentrate on making their health as good as possible without surgery.

Those who decide to go ahead may have a difficult wait for their new organs. Will they come in time? What will it be like living with a bleeper and knowing that if it goes off you must drop everything for major surgery? Will the operation work?

Both lungs are usually transplanted because drugs used to prevent rejection will suppress the immune system, so any bacteria in a diseased lung are likely to infect the whole body if the lung is not removed.

73

Since there is a continuing shortage of all organs
for transplantation, surgeons are trying out new
procedures, including live-donor operations.
Living-related lobar lung transplantation was first
attempted in California, but is spreading to the UK.
It relies on the fact that, owing to the difference
in size of chest cavity between people with CF and
those who do not have the disease, a lower lobe
of lung from a healthy donor can replace an entire
lung in someone with CF.

During living-related transplants, two living donors
donate the lower lobe of one of their lungs (one
from the right and the other from the left lung) and
these are used to replace the lungs of the individual
with CF. Clearly, the tissues must be well matched,
and parents or siblings are likely to be the most
suitable donors.

However, living-donor operations are major surgery
and have risks for donors as well as recipients.
So people need extensive information about
the operation and follow-up before agreeing
to take part. Transplant teams must be convinced
that everyone is happy with the arrangement and

no undue pressure is being put on donors or recipients to go ahead.

Only a small number of living-related lobar transplants have been carried out. But results to date compare favourably with those from conventional lung transplants.

Box 4
Criteria for Lung Transplantation in CF

FEV_1 – 30% of predicted value or less

PO_2 – 7.3 kilopascals (kPa) or less

PCO_2 – 7 kPa or greater

Estimated life expectancy less than 24 months (without transplant)

Substantial limitation of daily activities

Abbreviations:
FEV_1 forced expiratory volume in 1 second
PO_2 partial pressure of oxygen
PCO_2 partial pressure of carbon dioxide

Transplantation is not advised in people with:
• Significant disease of other organs
• Active infection in areas other than the lungs
• Poor nutritional status
• Current cigarette smoking
• Significant psychological problems

Box 5
My transplant
Lesley Saunders

I was 19 before I was diagnosed with CF.
My chesty cough had always been put down
to bronchitis or asthma and it was only when
I was older that I thought I really ought to get
this coughing sorted out. The sweat test was
positive and about two years later I developed
pancreatic problems.

From the age of 21 I was in hospital more and
more often; I was medically retired from my
job in NHS administration and at the start of
1997 I had a collapsed lung after which I was
assessed for a transplant.

I had always known that, with CF, I could die
or end up needing a transplant. But, because
I was diagnosed late with a mild form, I never
thought it would happen to me. When it was
suggested that I have a transplant, I didn't feel
I could say 'no', but I assumed I'd have to wait
for ages.

In fact, it took about six months and by that
time I was on oxygen most of the time. I was
planning to get married at the end of November,
but the organs came up about a week before.
At first I said 'no, I'm getting married!' But I
knew the wedding could wait and I might not
get another chance at a transplant.

I had a heart/lung transplant and the operation
went very well. Two or three weeks later I was
ready to go home when I started getting back
pains which turned out to be osteoporosis.
I was also losing weight and was really not
very well. But about six to eight months after
the transplant, I turned the corner, started piling

on weight and have never looked back.

I never imagined I would get back to the way
I used to be – able to do whatever I want.
But I have. I even check the scar sometimes
to be sure I was ever that ill. I don't need any
physio now, though I take as much exercise
as possible.

I take anti-rejection drugs and I've had to
get used to the fact that I pick up every cough
and cold going around. But whereas I would
have been out for weeks with an infection
before the transplant, now I bounce back in
a few days.

My husband Paul and I probably won't have
children because of the effect it might have on
my health, but we may consider adopting or
fostering in the future. A transplant is a scary
operation but, when I see some of the people
at hospital who have not done so well, I realise
how lucky I am.

Box 6
The family's story
Helen Douglas

James and I met at school when I was 16.
We did general studies together and I followed
him around asking for coffee, even though I
didn't drink the stuff. He was always coughing
and I heard that he'd got some dreadful disease
from which everyone died young. I never gave
it a thought.

We didn't really talk about what CF might
mean, even when we decided to get married
when we were in our early 20s. It didn't really

affect us until we were on a ski-ing holiday about 10 years ago. James had trouble getting up the mountain. Then, when we got home, he became too ill to take our daughter out. Eventually, he was at a conference and had to leave and go to hospital. He ended up in hospital for about 18 months and it was suggested he have a transplant.

I never doubted that James would get a new heart and lungs and that he'd get better. I've always felt that once you give up and become negative, things start going wrong. It was especially hard for James' parents because he was their third child with CF and the other two had already died, one in infancy and one at 13.

James' transplant changed our whole view of life. We have different priorities and we want to cram as much as we can into life. We now have four children and James started his own business so he wouldn't be ruled by a 9–5 day. He doesn't need to do anything for his CF now, apart from Creon, but he takes huge quantities of drugs to prevent him rejecting his transplant.

The children know about CF and they think of his scar as a big zip. They call him a druggie because of all the tablets he takes. But they're too young to remember how he ill he was. We were recently told that James is one of the longest survivors of a transplant, and that sounds like he's on borrowed time. But we don't think of it like that, we're just getting on with our lives and doing all the things we want to.

Gastrointestinal Complications

Gastrointestinal complications of CF include distal intestinal obstruction syndrome (DIOS), intussusception, appendicitis, pancreatitis, gastro-esophageal reflux disease (GORD), liver disease and gallbladder disease[27].

Distal intestinal obstruction syndrome (DIOS)

DIOS occurs more frequently among adults with CF than children. They get repeated episodes of complete or partial intestinal obstruction, often with colicky abdominal pain, bloating, and possibly constipation. DIOS may occur if pancreatic enzymes are stopped or following a respiratory exacerbation, dehydration, or a change of diet. DIOS rarely occurs in people who are pancreatic sufficient (i.e. who produce enough enzymes for digestion).

Mild episodes of DIOS may be treated with acetyl-cysteine sachets and a laxative such as polyethylene glycol or lactulose. Treatment continues until stools are passed normally, symptoms improve and any abdominal mass has disappeared. Special enemas (e.g. Gastrografin) that draw water into the bowel may also help.

Medical treatment is usually successful, although it may take several days for symptoms to disappear. If there is a complete obstruction and drug treatment is ineffective, surgery may be necessary.

After the acute problem has been relieved, the pancreatic enzyme treatment should be reviewed: the dose may need to be increased and oral laxatives used. Acetylcysteine sachets may also be used to help break up mucus in the gut.

Intussusception

Intussusception of the small intestine is a condition in which one part of the intestine is drawn inside an adjoining part. It affects about 1% of people with CF, and can be chronic and recurrent.

In CF, the problem occurs at an average 10 years

of age and generally affects the ileum and colon.
In other words, the lower portion of the ileum
and the valve of the caecum pass into the ascending
colon. Symptoms include intermittent, crampy,
abdominal pain and bloody stools. Intussusceptions
can be reduced with an enema.

Acute pancreatitis

Acute pancreatitis, which follows blockage of the
pancreatic ducts and release of enzymes that damage
pancreatic tissue, is sometimes a problem in adults
with CF who are pancreatic sufficient. It can be
treated with analgesics for pain, intravenous
fluids, fasting, and possibly nasogastric suction for
2–4 days. Acute pancreatitis usually resolves within
3–7 days after treatment has begun.

Gastroesophageal reflux disease (GORD)

In gastroesophageal reflux disease (GORD),
partially digested food in the stomach pushes back

into the gullet, or oesophagus, resulting in a painful burning sensation and acid taste in the mouth. People with CF are susceptible to GORD because the muscle in their gut moves more slowly than normal, so there is more opportunity for food to be pushed back into the gullet.

People with CF are treated in the same way as anyone else with GORD. They are advised not to eat or drink things which may irritate the oesophagus, such as caffeine-containing drinks (coffee, fizzy drinks) and alcohol. The last meal of the day should be eaten at least 2 hours before bedtime, and the head of the bed should be raised.

Treatment with metoclopramide, antacids, H_2-receptor antagonists (such as cimetidine or ranitidine), or proton pump inhibitors (such as omeprazole) may help.

Liver disease

About 8% of adults with CF develop liver disease due to their CF, though the problem is uncommon in anyone under 15 years old. Small ducts in the liver become blocked with debris from disintegrating white blood cells and fibrous tissue forms in an attempt to repair the damage. This scarring of the liver impedes blood flow, resulting in an increase in blood pressure in the portal vein – a key blood vessel carrying blood from the intestines to the liver. This portal hypertension, coupled with cirrhosis, is seen in about 5% of adults with CF and can be very disabling or even fatal[28].

Other complications often accompany cirrhosis, including liver failure and enlargement of the spleen. Fluid may collect in the abdominal cavity, and swollen veins around the lower oesophagus may bleed. If you have any of these complications, you'll be treated in the same way as other people with these conditions and that may include liver transplantation.

To pick up signs of liver problems at an early stage, you're likely to be offered an annual blood test to check your liver function, and a scan of your liver and spleen every two years. Promising results have been reported following early treatment with ursodeoxycholic acid[29].

Gallbladder disease

Gallbladder disease and gallstones (most commonly cholesterol stones) are also complications of CF. Gallstones may be caused by an excessive loss of bile salts through the stools, although other factors probably also play a part. Treatment of gallbladder disease includes dissolving gallstones chemically or with shock waves, or surgical removal of the gall bladder. This may be done using minimally invasive (keyhole) surgery to reduce lung complications.

Diabetes Mellitus

Diabetes is a common complication of CF, especially in adults. About 5% of young people with CF, aged 11–17, have diabetes which needs insulin treatment, rising to 12% of 18–24 year olds and 15% of those aged 25–34[30].

People with diabetes either do not make insulin or do not use it properly. Insulin is a hormone which is produced by a part of the pancreas, called the Islets

of Langerhans, which gradually becomes damaged
in CF.

Common symptoms of diabetes are thirst, hunger,
weight loss and an excessive need to urinate,
but some people with CF do not get any obvious
symptoms of diabetes. Instead, tests will show
that there is too much sugar in the blood
and urine.

Glucose intolerance

Most people who develop diabetes have a condition
called glucose intolerance for several years before
their diabetes becomes obvious. This means that
they are slow to clear extra sugar from their blood,
and they gradually produce less insulin. People
with CF and glucose intolerance may notice a
deterioration in their general health. Their lung
function may decline and they may lose weight.
This is why teenagers and adults with CF have
regular blood tests to check for signs of glucose
intolerance or diabetes.

85

An oral glucose tolerance test (GTT) measures
blood sugar levels 2 hours after you drink a sugar-
containing solution. A blood sugar level above
11.1 mmol/l indicates diabetes. The test may be
repeated, especially if you have no symptoms,
as a raised level may be temporary and not need
treatment. It is usually also carried out on an annual
basis to assess glucose tolerance.

Treatment of CF-related diabetes

The usual treatments for type 1 and type 2 diabetes
have to be modified for people with CF.

For example, most people without CF who have
diabetes are advised to stick to a low-fat, low-calorie
diet. But adults with CF who develop diabetes
generally don't tend to do well with a low-calorie,
low-fat diet as it makes them lose weight. Instead,
they are advised to eat a high-energy diet with
35% to 40% fat, 20% protein, and 40% to 45%
carbohydrate. The daily intake may be divided into
three main meals and three snacks.

As people with CF and diabetes tend to produce less insulin, they are also advised to have insulin treatment. The dose of insulin needs to be adjusted to food intake, which may vary.

Complications of diabetes

People with diabetes can get complications, whether or not they have CF[31]. The most common of these complications is damage to the part of the eye where images are recorded – the retina. This is called retinopathy. Other complications include kidney, circulatory and nerve damage, but these can take years to develop, and may be prevented if you take care to control the amount of sugar in your blood.

However, you should have regular check-ups with a diabetes specialist to look for signs of complications.

Eating disorders

Eating disorders, such as anorexia nervosa and bulimia nervosa are a growing problem in the UK and, as they are often rooted in an individual's perceived lack of control of their life, it is perhaps not surprising that people with CF should be affected.

Those with anorexia nervosa eat so little that they become very thin, but they still believe that they are too fat and refuse to eat properly. Those suffering from bulimia eat large amounts of food in a short period of time and then vomit it up to avoid putting on weight.

Both conditions damage any or all of the major organs, and even kill. Symptoms of anorexia nervosa include constipation, stomach cramps and dizziness, while bulimia can cause acid reflux, intestinal problems and dehydration. Serious weight loss also leads to infertility and osteoporosis.

Some people become anorexic because they are terrified of being fat. They want the same thin bodies they see as beautiful in magazines and on television. Others use food as a way of dealing with emotional problems or to feel in control of at least one part of their life – eating.

There is no instant cure for anorexia and every case is different. Some get so ill that they need to be tube-fed to keep them alive. Less serious cases do not need such desperate treatment. But people usually need help to get back into a routine of eating regular meals containing the high-energy foods required by those with CF. This can be done in hospital or at a special unit for people with eating problems.

Anorexia treatment works best when people want to get better and agree that they need to put on weight. It is important to try and find out why someone has stopped eating. This usually means talking to the whole family, not just the person with anorexia.

People with anorexia can also have therapy to help them feel better about themselves and understand why being thin is not the answer to their problems.

Treatment of bulimia also depends on helping people to understand why they developed their eating disorder and to find less dangerous ways of dealing with them. They need to learn not to run to the 'fridge when they are anxious or unhappy, but to talk about their problems with someone close to them.

89

Joint and bone conditions

People with CF are prone to arthritis and other joint diseases. These include acute episodic arthritis which generally occurs in early adult life, hyper-trophic pulmonary osteoarthropathy, which is also more common among adults, and occasionally, rheumatoid arthritis[32].

Some people with CF get repeated attacks of episodic arthritis, and these aren't usually linked with exacerbations. Severe joint pain and stiffness are often accompanied by a rash and fever. The cause of this form of arthritis isn't known, but symptoms respond well to non steroidal anti-inflammatory drugs (NSAIDs).

Hypertrophic pulmonary osteo-arthropathy (HPOA) is an inflammation of the bones, arms, and legs, which can accompany chronic conditions of the lungs and heart. But it is uncommon. Symptoms include finger clubbing, bone pain or joint swelling and may get worse during exacerbations.

Osteoporosis

Bones are far from inert. They undergo a continuing cycle of growth, break down and repair, just like any other part of the body. Most adults with CF make less new bone than usual – a condition called *osteopenia*. This may lead to thin, brittle bones which are prone to fracture – a condition called *osteoporosis*[33,34].

Adults with CF are also at increased risk of osteoporosis because of the adverse effects on bone density of the steroids they take to control their lung disease.

Rib fractures are a particular worry for adults with CF as they can make physiotherapy more difficult which, in turn, increases the risk of chest infection. Leg, wrist and back bones may also break. Fractures and weakening of the vertebrae in the spine can lead to *kyphosis* – hunching of the spine – which can result in impaired lung function.

91

Recent UK research showed that 1 in 3 people with CF aged 15–52 years had had a bone fracture and a similar proportion had low bone density[34].

Two key factors affect your risk of osteoporosis – the peak amount of bone mass you manage to build up in childhood and early adult life and your subsequent rate of bone loss. This is yet another reason why it is important that children and young adults maintain as good a diet as they can, as this will help build strong bones.

People with pancreatic insufficiency do not absorb vitamin D properly and this, too, can affect their bone development. This vitamin is usually checked with your blood tests at annual assessment.

Sex hormones also play an important role in bone development and loss. Women become prone to osteoporosis after the menopause, unless they use hormone replacement therapy to put back the oestrogen which they have stopped making. Similarly, boys and girls with CF who reach puberty later than other children may lose out on bone development because they have less exposure to oestrogen and testosterone.

Bone building remains important throughout your 20s and 30s, so your bone density should be checked from early adulthood onwards. This can be done with a scanning technique which uses low level X rays, and regular scans can help identify high risk individuals. They tend to be people with poor lung function and low body weight.

Good nutrition and regular exercise are the key to keeping your bones strong and healthy. Calcium rich foods such as dairy products and fish are recommended, and regular vitamins supplements will help maintain vitamin D levels. A small amount of sunlight exposure will also help boost vitamin D production in the skin, though you should be careful if you are taking antibiotics that cause a photosensitive rash.

Weight bearing exercise helps bone accumulation in childhood and maintains bone mass in adulthood. Your CF team will also keep a close check on your steroid dose to ensure that it is as low as possible, to limit the effects on bone density. The adverse effects of steroids are a particular issue for transplant patients who need to take high doses

93

of these drugs to prevent rejection.

Recent studies with a group of drugs called
bisphosphonates, which are widely used to treat
osteoporosis in post-menopausal women, have
provided promising results in CF too[35]. Research
is also investigating the benefits of high doses
of vitamin D and calcium.

Pain

People with CF get aches and pains in many parts
of their body. Some of these are caused by everyday
illnesses and injuries while others are related to
exacerbations or complications of their CF.

In the latter group are pains arising from:
- Unusually frequent or harsh coughing following
  a respiratory exacerbation
- Blocked sinuses following airway infection
  (e.g. sinusitis)
- Bloating or blockage in the intestine (e.g. arising
  from lack of pancreatic enzymes or DIOS)
- Joint or bone damage (e.g. arthritis, osteoporosis).

Any pain which is severe or continues for more than a few days without responding to simple remedies from the chemist needs investigation.

In most cases, the solution lies in effective treatment of the underlying cause of the pain. For example, chest and sinus pain may disappear when the underlying infection is successfully treated with antibiotics.

Abdominal pain may be relieved when the intestinal blockage or other disturbance is sorted out. There is no cure for the causes of arthritic pain, but much can be done to relieve the underlying joint inflammation and destruction.

Chronic pain can be treated with a wide range of painkillers, from simple agents such as aspirin, paracetamol and ibuprofen, to weak opioids, such as codeine, and strong opioids such as morphine. Low doses of antidepressant drugs can also have valuable pain-relieving effects. Some people get relief from nerve stimulation methods such as TENS or acupuncture.

95

Don't suffer in silence. Like any other problem, pain needs to be checked out and treated. In some cases, this may require a referral to a specialist pain management team.

Continence problems

Urinary incontinence may be more of a problem in CF than previously realised, particularly in young women. A recent survey carried out at a CF centre in the UK revealed that two thirds of young women with CF had urinary incontinence[36]. Leakages were most likely to occur during coughing, lung function tests or physiotherapy, and ranged from small drips to complete emptying of the bladder.

Over 80% of women over 35 had a problem, but 64% of those in the 16–20 age group also experienced leaks. This compares with 4–12% of young women of a similar age who do not have CF.

A quarter of women only reported problems when their chest was bad, but this left three quarters who had problems regardless of the state of their chest.

Overall, a quarter of the women who took part in the survey used incontinence pads – double the rate in a non-CF population of women. Despite the fact that many women reported severe distress as a result of leakages, few sought help, mainly because of embarrassment.

It is thought that continence problems in CF are due to a combination of stress, urge and retention incontinence. But CF specialists hope that women who experience continence problems will overcome their embarrassment and seek help, so that more effective management can be developed.

Emotional aspects and declining health

People with CF get anxious and depressed – just like the rest of the population. In fact, they are two of the most common conditions which people take to their doctor. At least 1 in 5 people in the UK suffer from depression at some point in their life and, at any time, about one in 20 are clinically depressed[37]. Despite continued efforts to remove the stigma of emotional conditions such as anxiety and depression, people still struggle on at home, unwilling to admit that anything is wrong.

It's entirely understandable that if you're dealing with the increased stress of a newly diagnosed or worsening complication of CF you're likely to feel anxious or depressed. There's a fine line between the two conditions, and many people suffer a mixture of anxiety and depression.

Anxiety is often broken down into acute symptoms which occur in response to specific triggers, such as panic attacks and phobias, and a more generalised anxiety which never seems to go away. Both can be helped by the so-called 'talking therapies'.

Most GPs have arrangements with trained coun-sellors who can help you talk about your worries and fears. They can also teach you relaxation tech-niques to enable you to deal with difficult situations. Your CF team may have similar arrangements or they may have a specialist advisor for emotional upsets. This may be a clinical psychologist who is trained in a variety of techniques or a therapist who specialises in a specific method of helping you.

One commonly used technique is called *cognitive therapy*. In collaboration with your therapist, you consider how helpful or unhelpful your day to day thoughts and beliefs are. For example, if your heart is racing, it's much more likely that you've been taking some exercise or getting worried about something than having a heart attack.

A therapist who is trained in cognitive techniques will help you question your responses to the everyday ups and downs of life, and think through how these thoughts and beliefs impact on how you feel.

Cognitive therapy also helps people sort out the things that are worrying them. But the therapist focuses on how problems have evolved over a period of time and why you have had trouble dealing with them. Did things happen when you were younger which have affected the way you cope with problems now?

Cognitive therapy is designed to help you understand why some of your difficulties may be made worse by the ways you have developed to cope with them. The aim is to recognise how these coping strategies started, how they can be adapted and improved, and how your strengths and resources can be mobilised.

Family and friends can be a great help when you're feeling anxious or fed up, but sometimes they just don't know how. When you feel ready, you may want to include them in your sessions with your counsellor or therapist.

Once the channels of communication have been established, you will hopefully find it much easier to talk about your anxieties next time they get the better of you. Some people become comfortable doing this with those they feel close to, while others always prefer to talk to someone outside their immediate circle, who can perhaps take a more dispassionate view. There's no right or wrong way to deal with the emotional problems which can occur when you have an exacerbation. What matters is that you get the help which feels right for you.

Drugs play a relatively minor role in the treatment of anxiety. Doctors do not like to prescribe tranquillisers or sleeping pills for more than a few days. Taking them for longer periods can lead to withdrawal symptoms when you do try to stop.

Drug treatment plays a larger role in clinical depression or when the anxiety has a significant depressive component. A lot of people say they are depressed when they are really just a bit fed up. Conversely, some of the symptoms of depression are similar to those of CF, so people with the disease may not realise they are depressed.

Sufferers of clinical depression gradually lose interest in life and get no pleasure from anything they do. They often feel worthless. They can't concentrate and feel tired. They may lose weight and have disturbed sleep. Waking up in the early hours, worrying, and being unable to get back to sleep is quite common. People who are depressed often feel agitated and restless. Most of all, they can't imagine life ever improving – there doesn't seem to be any light at the end of the tunnel.

101

Anti-depressant drugs should always be used alongside counselling, cognitive or other talking therapies.

But some people get so low that they need a few weeks of drug therapy before they feel well enough to start talking about their problems.

Anti-depressants do not cause the withdrawal symptoms associated with many tranquillisers, so courses usually last for several months, and it can take a few weeks before you start feeling better.

Recovering from anxiety or depression takes time and commitment from everyone involved. There'll be progress and setbacks, and improvement comes step by step.

Loss and palliative care

With deteriorating health come feelings of loss – loss of mobility, loss of career prospects, loss of social life, loss of opportunities. Rarely discussed, but much thought about is the possibility of loss of life.

With so much general optimism about the improved outlook for people with CF you may find it difficult to bring up the subject of death. Some people feel

guilty about their need to talk about it – that some-
how they are letting the side down.

If there is no one on your CF team who feels
confident about talking about the difficult issues
surrounding the end of life, you may be able to
see someone who works in your local palliative
care team, hospice or Macmillan unit, or a spiritual
advisor.

These people spend a lot of time with people with
serious conditions who are nearing the end of life.
They don't exactly specialise in talking about dying,
but they won't shy away from it. They won't set the
agenda, but if you want to talk about what life and
death mean to you, they will help you. By the nature
of their work, they have thought more about life
and death than most people – and helped many
others consider how they want to spend the time
that is left to them.

Talking about the end of life and bringing it out into
the open helps people to plan. There may be things
you want to do, places you want to go, people
you want to talk to. You may want to ensure that

103

people, animals or possessions that you care about are well looked after. Many parents want to prepare letters, scrapbooks or memory boxes for their children to read and look at when they are older.

Younger people who know their health is deteriorating may want to change direction – take time out to travel, go on courses, spend time in special places – rather than stick to a life-plan they drew up when they were well.

Acknowledging death doesn't mean you're accepting defeat, it means you are giving yourself time to plan and the opportunity to say goodbye to those you care about in a way of your choosing.

Co-ordinated care of children with CF at specialist paediatric centres has played – and continues to play – a key role in the improved outlook for people with the disease. In fact, research has shown that people with CF who are treated at specialist paediatric and adult centres have better nutritional status and lung function than those who aren't[38].

In its recent Patient's Charter, the CF Trust has set out the essential health care that children and adults with CF should expect to receive – based on current best practice, as agreed by specialists from all over the UK[13].

Most of the estimated 4,250 young people under the age of 16 who have CF are treated at one of the 29 specialist paediatric CF centres recognised by the Trust in the UK. But, as the number of adults with CF approaches that of children with the condition, it is widely agreed that there is a very real shortage of specialist services for adults.

There are only 16 adult CF centres in the UK and, as a result, some adults with CF are still cared for by chest physicians with no specialist expertise in CF, while others remain within the paediatric CF service long after they should have moved on[39].

While many of the chest and digestive problems experienced by adults with CF are similar to those seen in childhood, the nature and severity of these and the other medical complications which develop with time mean that adults need a package of care which is significantly different to that for children.

With adulthood come new emotional challenges and personal responsibilities too. And these also affect the way in which care should be provided.

At paediatric centres, much of the information and support about daily CF care is channelled through parents since it is they who will be responsible for nutrition, physiotherapy and medication.

Adolescence brings growing independence and a need for young people to take over the responsibility for their everyday care. This means gradually establishing a routine to meet the respiratory and

106

nutritional needs of young adults with CF, but within the context of normal, often chaotic, teenage life.

At adult centres, there is a shift in focus from parent as carer to patient in charge.

Approaching the transition

There is no right or wrong age to move from paediatric to adult care. Young people vary in physical and emotional maturity and those with CF are no exception. All big changes are a bit scary as well as exciting. You naturally feel confident and at home at the clinic you've been going to for years. You know the staff, the routine, the system.

You don't want to find yourself at an adult clinic before you feel ready, but nor do you want to wait so long that the move becomes a huge deal.

Most people with CF move from a paediatric to an adult centre between the ages of 14 and 18[40]. What's important is that, as you approach this time, your CF team and your family know how you feel

about it and when you think you are ready for
the change.

The doctors and other members of the team should
be making plans with you, not about you, and your
parents should be included provided that's what
you and they want.

The transition from paediatric to adult care should
be a gradual, planned process, not a one-off event.
The CF Trust has produced guidance on ensuring
a smooth transition[41].

You'll probably start talking about the move a year
or so before you are ready to go. That gives you
plenty of time to ask lots of questions about the
new place and how it works.

As you get older, you'll find that your paediatrician
is talking more to you, rather than to your parents,
about your CF and your treatment. This is how it
will be when you get to the adult centre. There may
be things you want to talk about privately with your
doctor or someone in the CF team. Your parents
may feel a bit rejected if you spring it on them in

the clinic, but if you mention it to them beforehand, they'll be more prepared.

Before you move to an adult CF clinic, you should also have the chance to meet some of the team who will be treating you in future. Hospitals vary in how this works. You may go and look around the adult centre or some of the team may sit in on a clinic at your paediatric centre.

At some places, this is done at a Joint Transition Clinic when you see both your paediatrician and the doctor who will be responsible for your adult care. The purpose of this is to discuss your medical care and help you feel confident about how you will be treated by the adult team.

Someone you get on well with from the paediatric team should act as your link with the adult team. They can arrange your visit to the adult centre and go with you, if you wish. They can also help with any worries you may have.

You should also be given an information booklet about the adult centre which explains how to get there, who the team members are, and what happens when you attend the clinic or are admitted to hospital.

If you are admitted, the ward you stay on should be suitable for you as a young person. You should feel happy about where you are sleeping and what you can do during the day. The staff should understand and respond to your emotional as well as your physical needs.

Box 7
The Transition
Sheredan Birch

Having Cystic Fibrosis has been second nature to me. I have known nothing else as I was diagnosed at just one day old. Going to the hospital every three months for a check up was very much a part of my life.

When my appointments were drawing near I would have sleepless nights worrying whether I had gained weight. Even on a hot summer's day I would wear as many layers of clothes as I could, so that the scales would tip in my favour. In case you do not know, one of the problems you have with CF is maintaining a healthy body weight. Whenever I walked into the consultant's room, I always felt as though I was being interviewed, where failure was not an option.

Turning sixteen, it was time for the move – from a child to an adult, from a girl to a woman and attendance at an adult clinic. Here I was introduced to another doctor, this time in another hospital. A very laid back, pleasant man, my kind of guy! For the first time in my life in a hospital appointment I was treated and spoken to like a person and not just a patient.

On the day of my first appointment at the adult clinic I was very nervous. I suppose you could say it was like attending a new school. I did not know them, they did not know me and when I was called from the waiting room my heart skipped many beats. Although I had already met my new doctor at the Children's Hospital we were still strangers. However, after only a few minutes I felt I had known him for years. We talked about anything and everything, whilst not forgetting the real reason I was there. My weight now was no longer the big issue, important yes, paramount no. My clinic appointments were now comfortable not critical.

After our meeting, my new doctor gave me a tour of my new ward. Unfortunately, at the sweet age of sixteen, a ward full of over 60s was not my idea of fun. Fortunately two years passed with only one hospital stay. My doctor was then given funds to set up a new unit based at another hospital. Although worried by this news I decided to follow him. It worked in my favour – less travel with the same level of care, if not better.

I had just got comfortable with my new hospital, when my doctor said he had been offered a new post elsewhere. I thought it was good for him but bad for me. That was until I was introduced to his successor, who I found to be just as approachable. Now two years later at the age of 26, the level of care is constantly improving and I feel this is due to the staff working as a team.

I am also fortunate that I have tremendous support from my family, friends and hospital staff (who I also count as my friends) and although living with CF is no fun, my life is made much easier by their much appreciated help, support and dedication.

I dedicate this piece to my family, friends and Andi, my loving husband.

Adult services

Arrangements for the treatment of adults with CF vary around the country. A few people will have most of their treatment at a CF Clinic at their local hospital, with annual visits to a specialist CF Centre, but most will receive all their care at a CF Centre.

The CF Trust considers that, with the growing complexity of CF care with increasing age, it is particularly important that adults with CF attend specialist adult CF centres.

It is essential that you have easy access to a range of people who specialise in the routine care of CF and its complications.

The CF team responsible for most of your care as an adult will be similar to that at your paediatric unit. There should be a senior doctor with a special interest in CF, a junior doctor (usually a registrar) who will know a lot about CF and may be planning a career in the specialty, and a dietitian, nurse, physiotherapist and social worker all with special experience of the needs of people with CF. A growing number of teams also have a psychologist to help with the emotional ups and downs which people with CF often experience.

At various times you may also need to see a specialist in one of the complications associated with CF, such as a gastroenterologist, diabetologist, a fertility specialist and/or obstetrician, a rheumato-logist or an orthopaedic surgeon.

These doctors should have expertise not only in their specialty as it affects the general population but also in the specific aspects that affect people

113

with CF. Such individuals may only be available at hospitals with major CF centres.

Routine care

Your CF team changes when you move to adult services but much of the care you receive will be the same as before. Your GP will continue to look after your everyday needs – appointments for minor problems and illnesses which are not due to your CF.

You will continue to have regular outpatient appointments every 2 or 3 months, depending on your health and your CF team. At each of these visits, your weight will be measured and you'll have a clinical examination. Your medication, diet and pancreatic enzymes will be reviewed and a sputum sample taken to check for infectious organisms. You'll also have some lung function tests and some-times an X-ray.

Annual review

Once a year, you'll have a full-scale check up, just as you did at the paediatric clinic. This is the time to review your progress, re-assess your needs and plan any changes to your treatment.

The main difference from an annual review at a paediatric clinic is that you, rather than your parents, will be asking and answering most of the questions. It's not an interrogation! But this is a great opportunity to have your say about the effects of your CF on your everyday life at college, at work, with your friends or with your family.

Are there changes you'd like to your diet, physio-therapy, exercise programme or medication which would make them fit in better with the other things you like doing? Are you having difficulty with any part of your treatment now that you, rather than your parents, are in charge? Are you anxious about anything?

Your annual review will include a check on your physiotherapy and nutrition, as well as your other drugs. There will be blood and lung function tests, and a chest X-ray, and some assessment of diabetes, usually a glucose tolerance test. Other tests such as an ultrasound scan of your liver or heart or a bone scan may also be arranged.

Inpatient care

A bed in a ward suitable for CF treatment should always be available at your CF centre. This should be in a room of your own to reduce the possibility of cross-infection.

The most likely reason for inpatient care is a respiratory exacerbation requiring lung function and blood gas tests, intravenous antibiotics and other medication. You will therefore need to be treated by doctors who are trained in setting up the necessary intravenous delivery devices and nurses who are experienced in checking and maintaining them.

When you are unwell, you may also need extra nutritional support to ensure your respiratory exacerbation does not have a 'knock on' effect on your overall health. So you'll also need ready access to a dietitian who specialises in CF.

Having to go into hospital for treatment can be depressing, especially if it isn't long since your last admission. You may want to talk about the way you feel with someone who is trained and experienced in helping with emotional problems. They won't be able to make all your problems evaporate, but a lot of people do find it helpful to explain how they feel to someone outside their family.

They won't tell you what to do, but they can help you consider the medical and practical options which are available.

Sex, fertility and pregnancy

CF has no effect on sexual function in men or women – they are no more likely to have problems with lovemaking than anyone else. Impotence is no more common in men with CF than the rest of the population and sexual difficulties are no more frequent in women with CF. So sexually active men with CF need to use condoms to protect themselves and their partners from sexual infection – just like anyone else.

Puberty may occur a little later in people with CF because they tend to grow more slowly, owing to their digestive problems. So men with CF may not reach their full height until they are 16 or 17 and women may not start their periods until they are about 14.

CF does affect fertility. In most men with CF, the tubes, called the *vas deferens*, which carry sperm from the testes to the penis are blocked. They still release seminal fluid when they have sex but it does not contain any sperm. The majority of men with CF are infertile.

Women with CF have normal ovaries and womb
and although the mucus in their cervix is a little
stickier than normal, this does not seem to make
it more difficult for sperm to reach their eggs.
As women who are underweight are more likely to
have irregular menstrual cycles and to ovulate and
have periods less frequently, the nutritional problems
associated with CF may affect fertility.

However, women with CF do produce healthy,
fertile eggs, and they do have children, so if you
don't want to become pregnant you should always
use effective contraception. Antibiotics can reduce
the effectiveness of the contraceptive Pill, so always
be sure to use additional barrier protection during
a course of antibiotics.

Box 8
Sex and CF
Sam Hillyard

Many years ago, I wrote an article called
Haemoptysis: Not an Ideal form of Seduction
in which I described how off-putting it can be
for a partner to be faced with a girlfriend who

coughed up blood at the mere possibility of a sexual liaison. Nine years on and the problem still haunts me, but numerous other obstacles also stand in my way of a night of passion!

We are afflicted with many complications which can jeopardise a healthy sex life: vaginal dryness (brought on by tension caused by 'will I cough, won't I cough?'), thrush (due to re-current antibiotic use), breathlessness, nausea, pain, coughing, tiredness, and haemoptysis; not to mention over-night feeds. If you're sensitive about how you look when undressed, this too can make it even more difficult to relax during intimacy.

When things are getting the better of us, Phil and I find it can help to laugh at things that frustrate us, and which we have no control over.

Since we 'got it together' I have developed a condition with means I occasionally have seizures, often resulting in loss of consciousness. I have no idea what I'm doing during this time. On recovery, Phil turns to me and says, 'Thanks for the blow job!' and I reply 'What blow job?' or if I think fast enough: 'You're welcome!' Having to improvise is frustrating, particularly when it means diverting away from sexual positions you find more pleasurable, or not being able to be as adventurous as you'd like. Some things just ain't fair.

However, when it comes to sexual alternatives, here are a few variation ideas to assist with the following:
- Breathlessness – Some positions are more comfortable than others, and less likely to make you short of breath.
- The same goes for coughing and/or haemo-ptysis, but both can also be brought on by the

whole exercise element. If so, try taking a less active role. That does not have to mean less participation – as I'm sure your partner will confirm, a lot of stimulation can be achieved with hands and fingertips.

• *If you are able* to relax completely despite restrictions, then stroking and/or massage can be great on its own and/or to achieve a climax, as well as a lead up to gentle love-making.

• Mild thrush – If you have a mild case of thrush (i.e. not in discomfort) sex is not out of the question. But you'll need to use condoms – not only to protect your partner from catching it, but also because if they do pick it up it'll just come straight back to you once you think you're in the clear. Be warned! Like many sexually transmitted diseases, not everyone displays the symptoms, but can pass them on regardless.

• Take the night off – If your inhibitions arise mainly because of overnight feeding or coughing made worse by unavoidably having to nebulise late at night, why not have a night off once in a while? I'm not encouraging blatant neglect of treatment, but I'm sure your consultant would agree that quality of life is important. So, if there are no *other* obstacles standing in your way: *seize the moment!*

• And yes, finally the key word. Lack of communication is the main source of problems in relationships, whether you have CF or not. Never forget – your partner is not a mind-reader!! . . . . . *IF ONLY!!!*

From *Input*, a magazine produced by adults with CF (Issue 26 Summer 2000)
© Sam Hillyard 2000.

Fertility treatment

Couples who have difficulty becoming pregnant can be referred for fertility treatment. You may have to pay for treatment, as it is frequently not available or very limited on the NHS. Most units operate some sort of age limit too.

The first step is to assess the nature of the problem. Infertility affects about one in seven couples, whether or not they have CF. So all the common causes of fertility problems need to be investigated, as well as those which are more frequent in CF.

Some couples with fertility problems choose to adopt, but *in vitro* fertilisation (IVF) techniques can be used to help women who fail to conceive and men who produce sperm but cannot release them in their semen.

Alternatively, some couples opt for artificial insemination with donor sperm (AID). Children resulting from this technique will be genetically related to the mother but not to her partner. The procedure is straightforward – donor sperm are carefully inserted into the woman's vagina at the most fertile time in her menstrual cycle. Pregnancy rates are in the order of 60–70%.

Sperm aspiration and ICSI

This is a relatively new technique which is proving helpful for men with CF who have fertility problems. Under local anaesthetic, sperm are taken directly from the testes. Eggs are taken from the female partner, usually through the vagina.

A single sperm is then injected into each egg, using a technique called intra-cytoplasmic sperm injection (ICSI). Fertilised eggs are then returned through the woman's vagina so that they can develop normally in the womb. About a quarter of such attempts result in a baby.

Pregnancy

If you have good lung function and are in good overall health, there is no reason why you should not have a successful pregnancy, but you'll want to discuss the practicalities with your CF doctor first.

Lung function is affected by pregnancy but every
effort will be made to maintain your respiratory and
nutritional status, usually with additional medicines,
nutrients and vitamins. This will mean more clinic
visits and more check ups.

In a small study carried out in the Midlands and
north of England, 18 out of 22 pregnancies in
women with CF were completed successfully,
producing healthy children who did not have
CF. Mothers lost an average 13% of FEV_1 during
pregnancy, most of which was regained. Six infants
were preterm and two were light for dates.
A subsequent larger review of pregnancies in women
with CF in the UK confirmed that most pregnancies
are successful but that outcome is linked to
maternal lung function[42].

If you're planning to get pregnant, you'll want to
talk about your physiotherapy and exercise routine
with your physiotherapist, and work out a plan
for the later stages of your pregnancy when it may
be more difficult to stick to your usual regime,
and you may therefore be more prone to infection.

Your physiotherapist may also need to be on hand during labour to help you with your breathing. You should be able to have any of the anaesthetics available to women in labour, but an epidural may make physiotherapy easier.

If your overall health is less good, you'll want to think very carefully about the long term effects of pregnancy on your well-being. An irreversible loss of lung function may have more far reaching consequences for you and your family.

Like anyone with a condition which affects life expectancy, all adults with CF will want to consider the long term impact of their condition on the welfare of their children as they grow up. Realistically, adults with CF may not see their children complete their education and make their own way in the world, especially if they start their family later in life.

Counselling is an integral part of fertility treatment in specialist centres. Women with CF who are planning to get pregnant may also want to talk to someone who understands the dilemmas of parenthood as they affect people with CF. There may

be someone in your CF team, such as a clinical

psychologist, who specialises in such issues or you

may be referred to someone linked to the local

obstetric or fertility service.

Such opportunities vary around the country and you

may need a referral further afield to get the kind of

help and support you are looking for.

Box 9
My pregnancy
Joanne Baker

My experience of pregnancy was quite a good
one. I had a few difficult weeks when I had to
stay on bed rest but, on the whole, it was a very
easy time.

Before I became pregnant I was the healthiest
I had been in a long while. I was working out
in the gym three or four times a week and I had
not needed IVs for quite a few months.

I found that I was pregnant at about six weeks
and gave my consultant a really hard time
making sure that all my medication was safe
to take. I had regular IV treatment to keep
me as well as possible and the only problem
that I encountered was with my physiotherapy.
I suffered a lot of indigestion and, once I got
to about six months, I found it uncomfortable
to tip the bed during physio.

I was very fortunate to have excellent obstetric care. I was told at my first appointment that I would probably have the baby six weeks early by Caesarean section, although the consultant would assess me nearer the time.

On Friday, 9th February at 9.50am, my daughter was safely delivered by Caesarean – a very healthy 5lb 5oz. She had a few days in intensive care but never gave us any cause for concern.

I, on the other hand, was feeling quite chesty and I asked the physio to come and see me. Because I had had a Caesarean, they would only let me do some breathing exercises – a bit like the active cycle. By the Monday I was feeling poorly and my chest consultant said I needed IVs. I had to move back to the CF centre for them and I was distraught at having to leave my daughter in hospital in Liverpool whilst I was in hospital in another part of the city. However, I knew that I needed to be at my healthiest for taking Eleanor home, and I eventually agreed.

I only needed one week of IVs and during that time I was allowed to go and visit Eleanor whenever I wanted. I went home and prepared the house for her and, at 18 days old, Eleanor was finally allowed home.

Although I had a very easy time with my pregnancy, I decided not to have any more children. The obstetric consultant said that if I was to have any more children he would prefer I had them straight away. I discussed this with my husband and we felt that 'healthy' women cannot always cope with two children under the age of two.

Also, if I needed to go into hospital for IVs in

the future, my Mum would be the main carer for our children. I felt that she wouldn't mind looking after one child, but it was too much to ask her to look after two or more. So eventually we decided that I should be sterilised, and this was done when Eleanor was 12 months old.

I have never regretted my decision not to have any more children. I have one very healthy and adorable daughter and I have been extremely lucky that I suffered no deterioration to my health in having her.

Box 10
Being a parent
Andrea Armitage

Having my two children were the two best decisions I ever made and the two best reasons I can think of for trying to keep myself well. Having said that, being a parent is also the hardest thing I have to deal with in my life.

Living with CF and being a parent raises several immediate dilemmas:
• how do I tell the children?
• how much detail do I give them about the treatments and the future?
• what is the right amount of information and what will they find frightening?
• when do I tell them about the genetic nature of the disease and the implications for their adult lives as carriers of the CF gene?
• how do I cope with the guilt of exposing them to all of the above?

If I had to list three things that I was unprepared for before becoming a mum, they would be how much I love them (fiercely!), the guilt complex (totally unrelated to my Catholic upbringing), and how much more mortal I would feel (I want to be the one who is there for them).

I think my children are what drive me, more than ever, to look after myself and keep well.

Right from the start I decided to have an honesty policy with my children. CF is a part of me and so it has to be a part of our normal family life. For this reason I have been very open about my CF and it is not special or different for them at the moment (they are seven and four). I am just their mum and I am how I am.

From being toddlers I have involved them in my care. From a crawling position they have eyed my compressor with interest and played with the elephant tubing, taking out the last of the ornaments as they swung it around! They have 'helped' me piece the nebuliser back together, 'borrowed' syringes for bath-time fun and tottered over to pat my back when, having laughed too hard at their antics, I have descended into a coughing fit!

Before nursery and school days began they accompanied me on each clinic visit. I wanted them to be familiar and comfortable with a hospital setting, staff in uniforms and technical equipment. I decided that if these things had to be a part of their lives then I did not want them to be threatened or scared by any of them. I have given them the basic facts as simply as I can and I try to be led by their questions now.

I love my children and I treasure my time with them. I want to experience things and teach my kids so much – now! I don't want them to miss out on anything, or me either. It's not that I'm pessimistic about the future, but just in case my health does fail (and it need not be the CF), I want them to have lots of memories of us as a family and of special times. I want them to always know that they were loved.

I have a little box on my dressing table. The kids call it 'mummy's treasure box'. It contains items special to me that, one day, I hope will be special to them. The hospital wrist bands from when each of them was born, first photographs, locks of hair, first teeth lost, and so on.

I have also made plans for their upbringing which, I hope, will never have to be put into place. It is a relief to know that these tasks have been dealt with and, in a strange kind of way, it gives me peace of mind. It leaves me free to enjoy the now, which is what counts most for the children too. Life is good!

Adults with CF vary so much in how they are affected by their condition that many do not consider that they have a disability. However, under the 1995 Disability Discrimination Act, people with progressive impairments, such as those which can occur in CF, are eligible for a range of practical and financial measures to support them during further education and when they start work. In addition, the Act aims to ensure that people do not experience discrimination in other areas of daily life, such as buying a home and getting insurance. The social workers who are part of your CF team will be able to help and advise on many of these issues.

It is up to you to decide who you tell about your CF and when you tell them. But if, for example, you fail to mention your CF when you get a job, you may lose some legal rights relating to the Disability Discrimination Act or unfair dismissal. Whenever you discuss your CF, it is important to explain how your CF might affect you at college, at work, or in everyday life, and to talk about your strengths.

131

Further education

Like anyone planning further education, your choice of college will depend on the type of course you want to take, the other facilities and attractions which are available, and the part of the country where you would like to spend the next few years.

If you have CF, you will also want to consider how easily you will be able to get to classes and the type of accommodation you need to fit your physiotherapy and drug regimes around your lectures and social life. Will you be able to live in a no smoking building, get a room on the ground floor, and have access to en suite bathroom, self catering and a secure 'fridge in which to keep your medicines? Will your room have enough power points for your nebuliser and facilities for intravenous equipment?

You will also want to consider how close you will be to a CF centre and the suitability of the college sick bay for CF treatment. Under the Disability Discrimination Act, all places of higher education must submit a Disability Statement, outlining their provision for students with a disability, and future plans. You can compare what's on offer at http://cando.lancs.ac.uk/.

As a student with CF, you may be eligible for additional financial support to help you afford a decent place to live, high-energy meals – and a taxi home after a wild party! The Disabled Students Allowance is paid through your local funding authority (e.g. local education authority) and depends on your needs.

Once you have a college place, it's a good idea to discuss how your CF affects you with your course leader, so allowances can be made for coursework deadlines and examinations if you are going through a bad patch of health. You'll need to register with a college GP and it's useful to have a chat with the campus pharmacist about keeping emergency supplies of medicines you cannot do without.

For more detailed information, contact the CF Trust for a Higher Education Pack, which includes guidance for tutors and accommodation officers.

Box 11
A word of caution . . .
Teresa Jacklin

Ah youth! I used to go clubbing four times
a week and could still bounce into college
at 8.30 am with a bizarre lack of hangover.
I referred to the years between 18–21 as my
'early retirement' because I didn't think I'd
make it to the real one.

In fact I was under the impression that irrele-
vant of my excellent health I could take a turn
for the worse and drop dead at any moment.
Plus there was no point in planning a career,
as I wouldn't make it to 30 (the average life
expectancy was around 20 at the time). So I
went about the very serious business of having
fun. To be honest considering what I got up
to it's a miracle I'm alive at 34 let alone have
a good lung function.

Of course these days it's a different story.
Clubbing is still my favourite form of exercise
but I feel rough the next day even if I don't
drink any alcohol. My chest is affected by the
smoke and dry ice. So I just don't go if I have
anything important to do the next day. And by
the time I realised I wasn't going to die I was
no longer well enough to work 40 hours a week
which has restricted my job options. But, if I'd
qualified earlier, I could have easily switched
to part time work.

I suppose I am trying to say that everything
has consequences. If you are sensible you weigh
up the benefits of doing things against the
potentially long-term costs. Having a rebellious
cigarette at 15 is one thing, but trying to quit
when you want to get on the transplant list
at 25 is another thing entirely. Don't let being

sensible stop you having fun, but being sensible occasionally means you may live longer.

Taking the disease into consideration does not come easy for most people with CF. The gene for fighting spirit is also located on chromosome 7 and that can make it hard to cut yourself some slack. It may be worth spreading your 'A' levels out rather than trying to get them all at once. Your degree may take a year or two extra. Difficult and annoying decisions but they may be worth it if you have your health when you graduate.

If your specialist goes pale when you explain your dream job e.g. mountaineer, pilot, etc, perhaps you should explore other options. Figure out why you are attracted to the job e.g. the risk of falling off, and then look for other jobs that contain those aspects. Going for a safer option will mean that you can keep the job longer if your health declines. However if your life will be empty without the Himalayas then you should go for it. At least you will have some entertaining stories.

What about cross-infection?
Infections are another problem. I've turned down the opportunity to work with people with AIDS, as my pseudomonas would pose a health risk to them. Ditto with avoiding fellow hospital inmates on chemotherapy.

I thought long and hard before I got involved with CF voluntary work because of the inherent risks. The UK has some of the most stringent cross-infection guidelines but other countries that were not hit as badly by cepacia do not take the problem as seriously. Plus, at conferences, people with CF attending in their professional capacity, e.g. doctors, physio's, etc,

do not have to produce evidence of their micro-
biological status. You also have to consider
that a sputum culture will not necessarily be
accurate. You may be incubating an infection
in a tiny part of your lung and many labs are
inaccurate in identifying CF bacteria due to
inexperience. So even cross-infection guidelines
cannot guarantee safety.

People with CF have to act responsibly, but
doing so requires knowledge. You have to know
exactly what bacteria you are carrying in case
you meet another person with CF. You also
need to know how bacteria are transmitted,
e.g. cepacia via the air and MRSA via direct
contact. If you don't know how an infection
is transmitted ring your hospital and ask.
If your doctor doesn't know, ask to speak to
the microbiology department. They won't mind
you asking.

We need to be mature and discuss infection
status at the earliest opportunity so we can
minimise the risk of cross-infection. You also
need to remember that emotional factors are
involved and not everyone can be trusted to
act responsibly. Try to consider other people's
feelings. If someone doesn't know their infection
status point out that they should find out and
talk to them from at least 5 foot away. Don't
run out of the room screaming. If someone does
run out of the room screaming try to remember
that they are acting from fear or ignorance
and it has no bearing on you. Fear is a very
powerful emotion.

Most importantly, please remember that new
infections are constantly emerging and spreading in the CF population. It is only a matter
of time before one that has a potentially more
serious impact than cepacia appears. Hopefully

when it does we will all be so clued up on cross
infection it won't result in unnecessary deaths.

What this all amounts to is we have to grow up.
Unfortunately the days when we could safely
snog someone with CF are long gone. Children
with CF need to be educated so that they understand when they can no longer play with Jenny
face to face and have to phone her instead.
Until they are old enough to take responsibility
for themselves their parents have to ask the
difficult questions.

But do the risks outweigh the benefits? You
can't help making friends if everyone else on
the ward is over 70 and is as much fun as a wet
haddock. The truth is peer support is invaluable
and we have a need, and a right to information
on CF. People who don't have CF can never
really understand what it's like to have such
a disease; therefore everyone needs to talk to
someone else with CF eventually.

Yes, other people with CF understand and are
willing to listen to you moan about the new
junior doctor and while nodding sympathet-
ically. But for me having friends with CF is so
much more than that. It's NOT having to ask
for things and NOT having to explain. They
won't make a drama if you become ill and will
trust you to let them know if they can do anything. You don't have to feel embarrassed about
the after effects of that 4-course dinner with
inadequate enzymes. And you don't have to feel
guilty if you are too tired to clear up the mess
you helped to create. But for me, most of all, it's
other people with CF who really appreciate my
sense of humour. Usually because they have one
that's just as bad.

Employment

In the 1994 Association of Cystic Fibrosis Adults (ACFA) survey[2], three quarters of respondents had at some time been in full time employment and nearly half were currently paid employees. They worked an average 34 hours a week. Unfortunately, about a third thought that, at some time, they had been denied a job because of their CF.

Companies with 15 or more employees have to comply with the regulations contained in the Disability Discrimination Act. This requires employers to make 'reasonable adjustments' for people with a disability, such as facilitating wheel-chair access, being flexible about working hours and allowing someone with a disability to be absent during working hours for rehabilitation, assessment or medical treatment.

Employers who display the Disability Symbol have agreed that they will interview people with dis-abilities who meet minimum criteria for the job on offer. These employers have also agreed to ensure that employees with disabilities are encouraged to develop their skills and remain in work for as long as possible.

As a result of the disability legislation, disability organisations recommend that people with CF or other progressive conditions tell employers who are bound by the Act (i.e. 15+ employees) about their illness. Realistically, there may be some jobs which are not suitable for people with CF – and that doesn't just mean scaffolders and road builders. For example, working in health-related professions may be inadvisable because of the likelihood of exposure to infection.

When attending an interview it is important to focus on what you can do, rather than what you can't. It's up to you how much you tell a prospective employer about your CF, but providing information tends to dispel anxieties rather than add to them. The varying nature of CF means that, although you may need time off work during exacerbations, you are likely to be able to work normally at other times. In fact the ACFA survey demonstrated low absenteeism amongst people with CF, with nearly six out of 10 respondents taking two weeks or less of sick leave in the previous year.

When you've been offered a job, you can clarify working practices – emphasising the need for flexibility. Your employer needs to be left in no doubt that you will be an enthusiastic and valuable member of staff who will work to your full potential.

The government operates various schemes to encourage employers to take on people with disabilities. Each Job Centre has a Disability Service Team which offers employment advice and an assessment service for people with a disability and their employers. Within this team, the Disability Employment Advisor will not only help you to find a job, but will also support you and your employer while you are working.

Your Advisor can also tell you about Access to Work – a government scheme which offers practical advice and support at work. This can include funding alterations to buildings, providing financial help for special equipment or travel to work, or funding a support worker.

Other government schemes are available which
enable people with disabilities to prepare for work
after a long period of unemployment or try out
a job for a probationary period during which the
employer receives help towards the cost of wages.
Details of these and other opportunities and benefits
are contained in the CF Trust's Employment Pack,
which also includes a factsheet for employers.
You can also get general information on benefits
by ringing the Benefits Helpline on 0800 882200.

Access to income

Whether you are in further education, paid employment or unable to work there are a number of
sources of financial help available to people with
CF both from the state benefit system and from
other agencies including the Cystic Fibrosis Trust.
Details of these and guidance on how to qualify for
them are contained in the *Guide to Financial Help*[43]
from the CF Trust.

141

The most commonly received benefit for people with
CF is the Disability Living Allowance (DLA). This is

for people who need help with personal care and/or getting around. Although there is no entitlement to DLA, many people with CF, including those in full time employment, have been able to claim this benefit at least at the lower rate. Your chances of success are increased if you seek help from the CF Trust's Regional Support Co-ordinators before filling in the appropriate forms.

Although adults with CF are not specifically exempt from prescription charges, those that do have to pay can purchase a season ticket to cover all their prescriptions for a year; current rates are outlined in the *Guide to Financial Help*[43].

Other sources of financial help

The Trust is itself able to provide some financial help to people with CF who are experiencing a particular difficulty at a time of stress or crisis related to CF. A small start up grant is provided for adults moving into their own homes and help can be given for holidays or respite care.

For more information on benefits and financial assistance contact your Regional Support Co-ordinator at the Cystic Fibrosis Trust (contact details shown on page 163).

CF and your home

The CF Trust has recently put together a comprehensive information pack about renting and buying your home. Much of the advice about avoiding the pitfalls involved in getting somewhere to live applies as much to those who do not have CF as those who do. However, some points are particularly relevant to people with a chronic condition such as CF.

Renting a council property

All councils must keep a register of people in the area who are waiting for a council home. The first step is to complete a Housing Application Form to assess whether you qualify to go on the register. Households which include someone with a particular need for settled accommodation on

143

medical or welfare grounds are amongst those which get priority for housing.

Most councils have special criteria for people who need to move because of serious ill health or a disability, and where health would be improved if they could be moved to another home. You will need to complete a medical form and the council's medical assessor will make a decision about your level of medical priority.

You will be informed of the result of your application including the number of points you have been given. This can be used to check that all your details have been taken into account. If you do not qualify to go on the housing register you will be given a letter explaining why.

Buying a property

Getting a mortgage is a stressful time for anyone. Repayment or endowment, fixed term or variable? You'll soon get to grips with the terminology if you get the CF Trust's information pack! Your health may become an issue if you need life assurance or other health insurance to ensure that your mortgage payments are kept up to date if you are too ill to work.

As with other insurance policies (see below), you may have more difficulty getting cover or have to pay higher premiums than people who do not have a serious illness. In the ACFA survey, two thirds of respondents who had applied for mortgages had restrictions placed on them by mortgage companies and/or insurers. Companies commonly insisted on joint mortgages or applied higher insurance premiums. One in eight responders had been refused a mortgage completely.

Getting insurance

The Disability Discrimination Act made it unlawful to discriminate against people with disabilities in connection with provision of goods and services. However, insurers are allowed to differentiate between apparently healthy individuals and those with disabilities in deciding whether they will provide cover and the premium they will charge.

They can ask you about pre-existing conditions, such as CF, and request information about the time you've spent in hospital, absence from work, and any disability requiring medical treatment.

It's very unwise to lie about your health in order to get insurance as this will invalidate any claim you make, and you will simply have wasted your money paying the premiums.

In many cases, companies are prepared to offer insurance but make exclusions for pre-existing conditions. This may be acceptable if you are wanting to take out travel insurance because there are plenty of non-CF reasons, such as theft of baggage or cancellation due to family problems, why you might wish to make a claim. However, the pre-existing conditions clause usually makes life or critical illness insurance less worthwhile, since the chances of your CF necessitating a claim are obvious.

Even so, it may be possible to get life assurance without exclusions provided you pay higher premiums. Most mainstream insurance companies give the rather non-committal answer that they take each case on merit.

For more information, ask for the CF Trust's Insurance Factsheet and/or the Holidays and Travel Abroad Information Pack.

Holidays and travel abroad

People with CF go on holiday like anyone else – in the UK and abroad. It's advisable not to travel alone unless you are sure you can cope, as you cannot expect tour reps or fellow passengers to take charge if something goes wrong.

You'll need to see your doctor about immunisations and medicines for your holiday and to obtain a medical certificate if your airline or insurance company has requested it. It's also worthwhile to check whether, in emergency, you can get your medicines in the country you are visiting.

All countries have some regulations about medicines

which can be brought in, and you can check this with their embassy in the UK.

To qualify for free or reduced cost emergency treatment in EU countries you'll need a form E111 which can be obtained, free of charge, in the leaflet 'Health Advice for Travellers' from the Department of Health Literature Line on 0800 555 777 or from main Post Offices and some travel agents. Be sure to apply at least a month before your trip. Health Advice for Travellers also contains information about reduced cost health arrangements in non-EU countries.

When you travel, take all the medicines you require for the trip, plus one additional week's supply. Prepare a stand-by supply of oral antibiotics in case of infection. Take extra enzymes in case food is high in fat, and be sure to pack sunblock if you are likely to need ciprofloxacin. People with CF are prone to dehydration, so take rehydration sachets if you are going somewhere warm.

Keep all your medicines in robust containers and divide them between suitcases, in case one bag goes astray in transit. The CF Trust can provide you with a standard letter explaining why you are carrying your medication. It is available in several languages, but allow three weeks for it to be prepared.

Before travelling, ensure that you can store your medicines in the right way at your destination. For example, you'll need a coolbag to transport your DNase and access to a 'fridge at your destination.

It is important to check with your doctor whether it is all right for you to fly as oxygen levels are lower in aeroplanes compared to those on land. If there is any concern, a special assessment of oxygen levels may be undertaken to see if you need oxygen during your flight.

If you need oxygen on your flight or at your destination, make sure your airline/hotel can provide it and check the cost of hire. If you need to use a nebuliser ensure you have the right adapters for the power supply. For more detailed information about how to make your holiday go smoothly, get the CF Trust's *Holidays and Travel Abroad Information Pack*.

149

About 1 in 12 cases of CF aren't diagnosed until people are at least 18 years old. This late diagnosis can occur for a number of reasons. The condition may be due to one of the rarer variations in the faulty CF gene, resulting in a mild form which is difficult to diagnose, or other genes may have helped to compensate for the harmful effects of the CF gene and masked the condition.

Symptoms of CF can be very variable; breathing problems may mimic those of asthma and bronchitis while digestive difficulties may be mistaken for inflammatory bowel disorders.

Unlike adults with CF who grew up with their condition, those who are diagnosed as adults need a crash course on CF and its management (the CF Trust has produced an information pack, specially geared to those who are diagnosed with CF later in life)[44]. Newly diagnosed adults quickly need to get used to physiotherapy, exercise and medication for exacerbations. If they have pancreatic insufficiency, they will need enzyme supplements and high energy foods.

Treatment should start as soon as possible and should be coordinated by a CF team specialising in adult care, with the same regular check-ups and annual reviews as required by all people with CF.

The need to incorporate constant medical care into everyday life is a major challenge for those who have a late diagnosis of CF. Research has shown that some groups of adults adapt better than others. Those who have always had some symptoms, and perhaps suspected they had CF, tend to be more familiar with the problems of chronic illness.

Although depressed about their diagnosis, they may be relieved that, at last, there is something they can do – in the form of exercise and physiotherapy – to improve their outlook.

In contrast, people who have never had any symptoms and had no reason to suspect they had a chronic illness tend to be more shocked and confused. They may deny their illness and avoid the recommended exercise and physiotherapy until they have noticeable signs of deterioration.

Coming to terms with a diagnosis of CF isn't easy
for anyone, and that includes partners, family and
friends. Many people who get a late diagnosis of
CF have already made decisions about the life they
want to lead. Some will be married or in long term
relationships, others will have started training
courses or careers which may be affected by CF.

The diagnosis forces an immediate rethink about
aims, expectations and responsibilities. Men who
want to have children discover that they will need
fertility treatment, while women find out that
pregnancy will need a little more care than they
had expected.

At some point, nearly everyone with CF is likely
to think about the longer term impact of their
condition on family and working life. Those who
are diagnosed late may find themselves having to
deal with these difficult issues at a time when they
are only just beginning to take in the much shorter
term problems of everyday healthcare.

The emotional stress of such a situation is bound
to put a strain on the strongest individuals and

their families. Sadness, disturbed sleep, poor concentration, loss of appetite and lack of energy are common – in both the person with CF and those close to them. Having an opportunity to talk things over, alone or with other family members, with a professional listener and/or others who have been through a similar situation can be immensely helpful.

The long term outlook for someone who is found to have CF as an adult is at least as good as for those diagnosed much earlier. The fact that symptoms have remained so well hidden or confused with another condition usually suggests a slower deterioration in lung and other organ function. But it is just as important to have regular checks for adult complications of CF, such as diabetes and osteoporosis, as for anyone else with the condition.

Box 12
They thought it was just the TB!
David West

My cystic fibrosis wasn't diagnosed until I was nearly 37. I had kept getting collapsed lungs and my sister had died of cystic fibrosis when she was 20. So I guess I'd always had it in the back of my mind. But I think it was my TB which put people off the scent!

That was diagnosed when I was 20 and serving in the army. The treatment cleared up the infection, but I was left with a lot of scarring on my lung and I retired from the forces. From then on, I always seemed to have a lot of infections and coughed up a lot of sputum. But it wasn't until after I had surgery to stick my lung back together in 1995 that I was finally tested for CF. I was coughing up so much mucus that they did a sweat test and it came back positive.

With hindsight, the CF explains a lot. For example, I had a nasal polyp in my teens and a very low sperm count. My son, Daniel, was born thanks to IVF. He's been tested and he's clear. But my younger brother has tested positive. So that's three out of us eight children who had CF.

Obviously, it would have been better if my CF had been diagnosed when I was younger. I might not have had so many health problems later on. But I've got used to the physio and the drugs and I believe in getting on with life. You can't change things!

I work three days a week now at an engineering firm and do some gardening, growing plants for sale, the rest of the time. I don't do any heavy work, but I can manage the plants.

My CF doesn't stop me doing things. I went to Canada recently for three weeks. Packed up my things, got my drugs together, and off I went. Of course, it helps that I am married to a nurse. She keeps me on track, if I ever forget my treatment. Life goes on, doesn't it?

Greater life expectancy, valuable improvements in current treatments, and early success with new therapeutic approaches make this a hopeful time for everyone involved with CF.

The ultimate objective for all of us is to be to able to correct the basic genetic defect rather than just treating the symptoms of the disease. An immense international effort is therefore focused on this goal. As researchers refine their skills in manipulating the CFTR gene and increase their understanding of the CFTR protein, they are taking the first important steps towards an eventual 'cure' for CF.

So far the emphasis has been on gene therapy – trying to replace the faulty gene with a healthy copy. By the middle of 2000, some 200 volunteers with CF had received some form of gene transfer into their airway cells. These trials have confirmed that it is possible to correct the biochemical and electrical faults in the cells which line the airways of people with CF. But the effects so far have been too weak and short-lived to be of clinical benefit.

155

Scientists are now back in the laboratory devising ways to overcome the natural barriers to gene therapy such as the thick mucus in the lungs, and to produce more potent forms of the gene and its carriers. Hopefully, future clinical trials will show that it is possible to turn molecular correction into symptomatic improvement.

But gene therapy is not the only promising approach to correcting the basic CFTR gene defect; another option is to try and repair or replace the faulty CFTR protein. The last few years have seen a rapid increase in understanding of how CFTR protein works normally and the different ways in which it is faulty in CF. As a result, new drugs which may correct these faults are starting to be tested in clinical trials. Other new treatments may result from the information generated from the human genome project and other genetic studies currently underway.

But how will today's adults with CF benefit from such research? They don't want to sit around waiting for a cure, they want to get on with life now.

Absolute assurances are difficult. Scientists and doctors attempting gene correction are optimistic, but treatment to prevent organ damage is likely to be most effective when given early in life. Even so, it is possible that genetic correction of moderate, and perhaps even more advanced disease, may arrest further damage and thus maintain current function and quality of life.

In the meantime, best treatment practices are continually being re-assessed and novel approaches to relieving symptoms investigated. The introduction of DNase is just one recent example.

Such work continues. Progress is being made with potent drugs to damp down the damaging inflammation in the lungs of people with CF. For years, doctors have been aware of the potential of a natural anti-inflammatory substance in the lungs, alpha 1-anti-trypsin (AAT), but until recently the substance has only been available in very small amounts. Now, the gene for human AAT has been stitched onto the gene for milk production in sheep and a flock of animals are producing AAT in their milk. Enough purified AAT from sheep milk is

157

now available for tests to start on people with CF.

Controlling infection is another critical area.
The whole of the genetic make up of the bacterium
most commonly associated with CF, *Pseudomonas
aeruginosa*, was recently unravelled. This will
provide important new information about its
virulence and resistance to antibiotics and should
indicate ways of getting around these problems.

Research is underway to reproduce peptide antibiotics against which bacteria do not readily develop
resistance; these peptides are found naturally in the
fluid which lines the airway surface. Attempts are
also being made to find substances which break
down the protective layer with which Pseudomonas
surrounds itself when it gets into the lungs.

Clearly, CF is under attack on all fronts, and the
imagination and resourcefulness of the research
teams are being rewarded. But the solutions to the
challenges of CF will not come from individuals.
Instead, they will continue to emerge from the joint
efforts of those with the disease, their families and
supporters and those who manage their daily care.

1. Standards for the clinical care of children and adults with cystic fibrosis. Cystic Fibrosis Trust. 2001.

2. Association of Cystic Fibrosis Adults survey. 1994. Unpublished.

3. Rommens JM, Iannuzzi MC, Kerem B-S, et al. Identification of the cystic fibrosis gene: chromosome walking and jumping. Science 1989; 245:1059–1065.

4. Riordan JR, Rommens JM, Kerem B-S, et al. Identification of the cystic fibrosis gene: cloning and characterization of the complementary DNA. Science 1989; 245:1059–1065.

5. Kerem B-S, Rommens JM, Buchanan JA, et al. Identification of the cystic fibrosis gene: genetic analysis. Science 1989; 245:1073–1080.

6. Davis PB, Drumm M, Konstan MW. Cystic fibrosis. Am J Respir Crit Care Med 1996; 41:431–451.

7. Burke W, Aitken ML, Chen SH, et al. Variable severity of pulmonary disease in adults with identical cystic fibrosis mutations. Chest 1992; 102:506–509.

8. Campbell PW, Parker RA, Roberts BT, et al. Association of poor clinical status and heavy exposure to tobacco smoke in patients with cystic fibrosis who are homozygous for the ΔF508 deletion. J Pediatr 1992; 120:261–264.

9. Rosenstein BJ, Cutting GR. The diagnosis of cystic fibrosis: A consensus statement. J Pediatr 1998; 132:589–595.

10. Epidemiological survey of bacteria isolated from the respiratory tract in European CF patients. Data from the European Registry for Cystic Fibrosis. XIIIth International CF Congress, Stockholm, 2000.

11. Valerius NH, Koch C, Hoiby N. Prevention of chronic *Pseudomonas aeruginosa* infection in cystic fibrosis by early treatment. Lancet 1991; 338:725–726.

12. A statement on *Burkholderia cepacia*. Cystic Fibrosis Trust's Infection Control Group. July, 1999.

13. CF Trust. The care of patients with cystic fibrosis. A Patient's Charter, 2000.

14. Clinical guidelines for the physiotherapy management of cystic fibrosis. Association of Chartered Physiotherapists in Cystic Fibrosis. October, 2000.

15. Elborn JS, Prescott RJ, Stack BH, et al. Elective versus symptomatic antibiotic treatment in cystic fibrosis patients with chronic *Pseudomonas aeruginosa* infection in the lungs. Thorax 2000; 55:355–358.

16. Szaff M, Hoiby N, Flensborg EW. Frequent antibiotic therapy improves survival in cystic fibrosis patients with chronic *Pseudomonas aeruginosa* infection. Acta Paediatr Scand 1983; 72:651–657.

17. Ramsay BW, Pepe MS, Quan JM, et al. Intermittent administration of inhaled tobramycin in patients with cystic fibrosis. N Eng J Med 1999; 340:23–30.

18. Konstan MW, Byard PJ, Hoppel CL, et al. Effect of high dose ibuprofen in patients with cystic fibrosis. N Eng J Med 1995:332:848–854.

19. Littlewood JM, Wolfe SP. Control of malabsorption in cystic fibrosis. Paediatr Drugs 2000; 2:205–222.

20. Prescott P, Bakowski MT. Pathogenesis of fibrosing colonopathy: the role of methacrylic acid copolymer. Pharmacoepidemiol Drug Saf 1999; 8:377–384.

21. Pancreatic enzyme supplements and fibrosing colonopathy. WHO Drug Information. 1996; 10:43–44.

22. Littlewood JM. Update on intestinal strictures. J R Soc Med 1999;92(Suppl. 37):41–49.

23. Antibiotic treatment for cystic fibrosis. Cystic Fibrosis Trust's Antibiotic Group. April, 2000.

24. Home intravenous therapy and cystic fibrosis. Advice for patients, parents and carers. Cystic Fibrosis Trust.

25. Abbott J, Dodd M, Bilton D, et al. treatment compliance in adults with cystic fibrosis. Thorax 1994; 49:115–120.

26. Aurora P, Balfour-Lynn IM. Lung transplantation and end of life issues in cystic fibrosis. Paediatr Respir Rev 2000; 1:114–120.

27. Littlewood JM. Gastrointestinal complications in cystic fibrosis. J R Soc Med 1992; 86 (Suppl. 18):13–19.

28. Sokol RJ, Durie PR. Recommendations for management of liver and biliary tract disease in cystic fibrosis. Cystic Fibrosis Foundation Hepatobiliary Disease Consensus Group. J Pediatr Gastroenterol Nutr 1999; 28 (Suppl. 1): S1–S13.

29. Columbo C, Battezzati, PM, Podda, M et al. Ursodeoxycholic acid for liver disease associated with cystic fibrosis: a double-blind multicentre trial. Hepatology 1996; 23:1484–1490.

30. Lanng S, Hansen A, Thorsteinsson B, Nerup J, Koch C. Glucose tolerance in patients with cystic fibrosis: five year prospective study. BMJ 1995; 311:655–659.

31. Lanng S, Thorsteinsson B, Lund-Andersen C, et al. Diabetes mellitus in Danish cystic fibrosis patients: prevalence and late diabetic complications. Acta Paediatr 1994; 83:72–77.

32. Lawrence JM, Moore TL, Madson KL, et al. Arthropathies of cystic fibrosis: case reports and a review of the literature. J Rheumatol 1993:20 (Suppl 38): 12–15.

33. Aris RM, Renner JB, Winders AD, et al. Increased rate of fractures and severe kyphosis: sequelae of living into adulthood with cystic fibrosis. Ann Intern Med 1998; 128:186–193.

34. Haworth CS, Selby PL, Webb AK, et al. Low bone mineral density in adults with cystic fibrosis. Thorax 1999; 54:961–967.

35. Haworth CS, Selby PL, Mawer EB, et al. Pamidronate increases axial bone density in cystic fibrosis adults. Pediatr Pulmonol 1999; Suppl 19:295.

36. Davis A, Unsworth RJ, Webb AK, et al. Urinary incontinence: a marginalised and untreated problem in females with cystic fibrosis. XIIIth International CF Congress Stockholm. June, 2000.

37. Royal College of Psychiatrists Factsheet No: 1. Depression: How common is it?

38. Mahadeva R, Webb K, Westerbeek RC, et al. Clinical outcome in relation to care in centres specialising in cystic fibrosis: cross sectional study. BMJ 1998; 316:1771–1775.

39. Conway SP, Stableforth DE, Webb AK. The failing health care system for adult patients with cystic fibrosis. Thorax 1998; 53:3–4.

40. Conway SP. Transition from paediatric to adult-associated care for adolescents with cystic fibrosis. Disabil Rehabil 1998; 20:209–216.

41. CF Trust. A Guide for Young People moving from Paediatric to Adult Care.

42. Edenborough FP, Mackenzie WE, Stableforth DE. The outcome of 72 pregnancies in 55 women with cystic fibrosis in the United Kingdom 1977–1996. BJOG 2000; 104:254–261.

43. CF Trust. Guide to Financial Help.

44. CF Trust. Late Diagnosis Pack.

**CYSTIC
FIBROSIS
TRUST**

Contact details:
Cystic Fibrosis Trust
11 London Road
Bromley
Kent   BR1 1BY
Tel: 020 8464 7211
Fax: 020 8313 0472
e-mail: enquiries@cftrust.org.uk
Website: www.cftrust.org.uk

Solvay Healthcare can be
contacted via their Cystic
Fibrosis Resource Centre on
www.cysticfibrosis.co.uk